英汉对照·心灵阅读

Sentiment
情感篇

董新颖　编译
林　立　审校

外文出版社

卷首语

总有一种感动无处不在。

总有一种情怀轻舞飞扬。

总有一种生活,在别处,闪动异样的光芒。

阅读,让我们的生活在情调与知性中享受更多……

故事与见闻,犹如生活的魅力与智慧,合着我们自身生命的光与影,陪伴我们一路前行。

快乐和圆满,幻想与失落,飞扬的眼泪,

行走江湖的落拓，不与人说的痛苦，渐行渐远的繁华，坚持的勇气，点点滴滴的小意思……

人生让我们感受到的，也许远远不只是这些；更多的是挫折后生长的力量，沉闷时的豁然开朗，是屋前那静静的南山上盛开的人淡如菊的境界，是闹市中跋涉红尘、豪情万丈的冲动，是很纯粹的一杯午后的香醇的咖啡……

漫步红尘，有彻悟来自他人的故事，有灵犀来自偶然的相遇，在这里，一种从未见过的却可能早就在我们心底的生活方式有可能与我们邂逅。

让我们一起阅读吧，感受生长的智慧、风雅与力量。

Contents
目 录

1. Mom / 1
   妈妈

2. Somewhere out there / 7
   此时彼地

3. The time account / 13
   时间账户

4. Our kind landlord / 19
   我们的好房东

5. A learning experience / 25
   学习的体会

6. The last relationship / 31
   分手

7. Life is a gift / 39
   生活本身就是一种礼物

8. Two interesting jokes / 45

   笑话二则

9. A father and a son / 51

   父亲和儿子

10. Speed skater tells story with heart and emotion / 59

    短道速滑手充满深情的故事

11. My one and only / 65

    我的惟一

12. An unforgettable Christmas / 73

    令人难忘的圣诞节

13. Dealing with anger / 81

    控制愤怒

14. A child's cry / 91

    孩子的呐喊

15. An unforgettable story / 97

    令人难忘的故事

16. The story of Julia / 103

    朱莉娅的故事

17. The potter / 109

  制陶工人

18. You sure are lucky / 119

  你一定会有好运

19. Return to Paradise / 125

  重返伊甸园

20. Destiny / 135

  前生注定

21. The best medicine / 143

  最好的药方

22. Is it worth the risk? / 155

  值得冒险吗?

23. A peculiar yet familiar feeling / 165

  一种特别又熟悉的感觉

24. My mother / 171

  我的妈妈

25. The color of friendship / 181

  友谊的色彩

26. The secret of happiness / 189
    幸福的奥秘

27. To feel better, you need to think better / 193
    心之所想,行之所依

28. Learning to accept yourself / 203
    学会接受你自己

29. The doll and a white rose / 215
    布娃娃和一枝白玫瑰

30. Best friends / 223
    最好的朋友

31. Love is memory / 231
    爱是记忆

32. Salty coffee / 241
    咸咖啡

33. Test of true love / 247
    真爱的考验

34. For the love of mother / 255
    献给母爱

Mom

妈 妈

She will be waiting for you and will take care of you.
Your angel will sing for you and will also smile for you every day.
Your angel will defend you even if it means risking its life.
You will simply call her Mommy.

她将等候并照顾你。
你的天使每天都会给你唱歌、向你微笑。
你的天使会保护你,即使会威胁到她自己的生命。
你只须简单地称呼她"妈妈"。

情 感 篇

Once upon a time there was a child ready to be born. So one day he asked God: "They tell me you are sending me to earth tomorrow but how am I going to live there being so small and helpless?" "Among the many angels, I chose one for you. She will be waiting for you and will take care of you[1]."

"But tell me, here in Heaven, I don't do anything else but sing and smile, that's enough for me to be happy." "Your angel will sing for you and will also smile for you every day. And you will feel your angel's love and be happy."

"And how am I going to be able to understand when people talk to me, if I don't know the language that men talk?" "Your angel will tell you the most beautiful and sweet words you will ever hear, and with much patience[2] and care, your angel will teach you how to speak."

"And what am I going to do when I want to talk to you?" "Your angel will place your hands together and will teach you how to pray[3]."

"I've heard that on earth there are bad men, who will protect me?" "Your angel will defend[4] you even if it means risking its life."

"But I will always be sad because I will not see you anymore." "Your angel will always talk to you about me and will teach you the way for you to come back to me, even though I will always be next to you."

妈 妈

很久以前，一个孩子即将出生。一天他去问上帝，"听说明天您将把我派往尘世，但是我弱小无助怎么在那里生活呢？""我在众多的天使中选了一位保护你。她将等候并照顾你。"

"但是，在天堂，我什么也不做，只要唱歌和微笑就会感到无比幸福。""你的天使每天都会给你唱歌、向你微笑，你会感到天使给你的爱，你会很幸福。"

"如果我不懂人类的语言，又怎么能听懂别人对我说的话呢？""你的天使将给你讲述你能听懂的最优美、最动听的语言，她会用耐心和关爱，教会你如何讲话。"

"我想和您谈话时怎么办？""你的天使会握住你的手，教会你如何祷告。"

"我听说在尘世中有坏人，谁来保护我呢？""你的天使会保护你，即使会威胁到她自己的生命。"

"但是我还会难过，因为我再也看不到您了。""你的天使会经常向你谈到我，而且会给你指引回到我身边的方法，即使我们相隔很近。"

❶ **take care of sb.**
照顾某人

❷ **patience**
/ˈpeɪʃəns/
n. 耐心

❸ **pray**
/preɪ/
v. 祈祷, 祷告

❹ **defend**
/dɪˈfend/
v. 保卫, 防卫

At that moment there was much peace in Heaven, but voices from earth could already be heard, and the child in a hurry asked softly: "Oh God, if I am about to leave now, please tell me my angel's name." "Your angel's name <u>is of no importance</u>[5]. You will simply call her Mommy."

妈 妈

天堂里一片安静祥和，但是来自尘世呼唤他的声音已经清晰可听，孩子连忙轻声问道："噢，上帝，我马上要离开您了，请您告诉我那位天使的名字吧。""那位天使的名字不重要。你只须简单地称呼她'妈妈'。"

❺ be of no importance
无关紧要

Somewhere out there
此时彼地

I am hopelessly in love with you, devoted to being with you. May God reunite us very soon. I am very hopeful that God will lead me to you once again.

不敢希冀再次和你相恋，不敢希冀把自己奉献给你，但愿上帝让我们重归于好，我企盼上帝再次把我带到你身边。

情感篇

Dear Paul

I know we are so far apart, and that has been months since the last time we were together. You would think that I have gotten better at not missing you as much. I can't explain how all this distance and time apart has made my love for you grow.

The last night that we were together, I took it really easy when we went out to eat. I had a great time talking to you and laughing when we spoke of our past times together. The day <u>passed me by</u>[1] and the control I had just vanished[2] slowly. When the night came and we found each other quiet in your car. I wanted to die because I realized that I still loved you so much, that I did not want to go home. I couldn't believe how you said you also wanted to see me at the time, but we were just too proud to call each other, and now I was leaving the next day. Yes, I broke into tears and cried in your arms after we just gave into our love for each other and broke away our pride and kissed. You cried with me, and those tears still remain saved in my heart. Though now they kill me every day, because I'm not near you.

I don't think anyone understands the burden I carry in my heart day by day ... until I am once again with you. I am hopelessly in love with you, <u>devoted to</u>[3] being with you. May God reunite us very soon. I am very hopeful that God will lead me to you once again. My first true love, I hope you feel the same, because it would be so much worse if I were lost in this feeling

亲爱的保罗：

我们远隔万里，已有数月没有见到对方了。你一定认为我现在过得很好，因为你觉得我不再那么思念你。但是，我也不明白时空的阻隔如何让我更加爱你了。

那一晚，我们在一起。我们共进晚餐，谈到了过去我们在一起的种种往事。我们谈笑风生地说了好久，时间过去了，我的自控力在慢慢消失。夜晚来临时，我们静静地坐在你的车上，我痛不欲生，因为我意识到我依旧那么爱你，我真的不想回家。我简直不敢相信你说的话，你说那时你想看到我，但是我们都太自负了，结果一个电话都没打。而我，第二天就要离开了。是的，当我们真情告白后，当我们撕下自负的面具后，当我们接吻后，我哭倒在你的臂弯里。你也哭了，那些泪水被我永远珍藏在心里，现在它们时常折磨着我，因为我离你是那么的遥远。

没有人理解我内心深处的伤痛，除非我再度和你再一起。不敢希冀再次和你相恋，不敢希冀把自己奉献给你，但愿上帝让我们重归于好，我企盼上帝再次把我带到你身边。这是我第一次真正的恋爱，我希望你也是这么想的。如果只是我一人在单相思，如果你丝毫没有思念我的情感，如果你从没有和我

❶ **pass by**
经过
❷ **vanish**
/ˈvænɪʃ/
v. 消失
❸ **devote to**
贡献

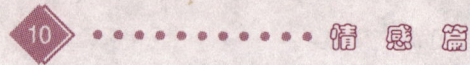

alone, without you to share it with and to share the thought of us being together again. I am sorry for all the bad moments and want to <u>make up for</u>[4] all our time apart. I love you, Paul.

Love always,
Joana

再到一起的想法，我的世界将一片灰暗。对于过去那些不愉快的日子，我感到抱歉和内疚，我真想补偿我们分开的那段时光。我爱你，保罗。

永远爱你的
乔安娜

❹ **make up for**
补偿，弥补

The time account
时间账户

Yesterday is history. Tomorrow is a mystery. Today is a gift. That's why it's called the present!

昨天已成为历史，明天仍是未知。只有今天才是礼物，这也就是我们为什么称它为"现在"。

SAY there is a bank that credits[1] your account each morning with RMB 6,400. Every evening, the bank deletes whatever remains of this sum that you have failed to use during the day.

What would you do if you had such an account?

Draw out every cent, every day, of course!

Well, each of us has such an account. Its name is TIME.

Every morning, Time credits you with 86,400 seconds. Every night it writes off, as lost, whatever you have failed to put to use. It carries over no balance. It allows no overdraft.

Each day, Time opens a new account for you. Each night, it burns whatever remains in the account. If you fail to use up all of the day's deposits[2], you can't keep them for tomorrow. Neither can you draw from what will be put in the next morning.

Time's clock runs non-stop.

To realize the value of one year, ask a student who has failed a grade.

To realize the value of one month, ask a mother who has given birth to a premature[3] baby.

To realize the value of one week, ask the editor of a weekly news-

时间账户

如果说有这样一个银行，每天早上都给你汇入 6400 元；每天晚上，都会清除你在这一天没有花完的账户余额。

如果你有这样一个账户，你会怎样做呢？

当然是每天都要取出每一分钱！

其实，我们每个人都有这样的一个账户，它的名字就叫时间。

每个清晨，时间都会为你开启一个拥有 86400 秒的账户；每晚，便会勾销一切你没有充分利用的时间，它从不延缓进出平衡，也不允许透支。

每天，时间都会给你开启一个新账户；每晚，都会清除账户上的余额（时间）。如果你没有用尽当天的时间存款，你也不能留着以备明天之用，而且你也不可能预支第二天的时间。

时间永不停息地奔跑着。

想要明白一年的价值，去问问留级的学生。

想要明白一个月的价值，去问问早产的母亲。

想要明白一周的价值，去问问周刊的编辑。

❶ credit
/ˈkredɪt/
v. 存入账户

❷ deposit
/dɪˈpɒzɪt/
n. 储蓄

❸ premature
/ˌpreməˈtjʊə/
adj. 早熟的

paper.

To realize the value of one hour, ask two lovers who are waiting to meet.

To realize the value of one minute, ask a traveler who has just missed his train.

To realize the value of one second, ask the motorist who has just avoided an accident.

To realize the value of one millisecond[4], ask the athlete who has won a silver medal in the Olympics.

Treasure[5] every moment that you have! And remember that time waits for no one. Yesterday is history. Tomorrow is a mystery. Today is a gift. That's why it's called the present!

时间账户

想要明白一个小时的价值，去问问正在等候见面的热恋情侣。

想要明白一分钟的价值，去问问没赶上火车的旅行者。

想要明白一秒钟的价值，去问问躲过交通事故的司机。

想要明白千分之一秒的价值，去问问在奥运会上获得银牌的运动员。

珍惜你现有的每一分钟吧！记住，时间不等人，昨天已成为历史，明天仍是未知。只有今天才是礼物，这也就是我们为什么称它为"现在"。

④ **millisecond**
/ˈmɪlɪˌsekənd/
n. 千分之一秒

⑤ **treasure**
/ˈtreʒə/
v. 珍爱，珍惜

Our kind landlord
我们的好房东

He also taught me an important lesson about not judging a book by its cover.

他给我上了极为重要的一课,那就是不要从书皮去鉴定一本书的好坏!

情感篇

Two friends and I moved into a house off campus when I was a junior at Iowa State University. We were all a bit afraid of our landlord, a gruff middle aged man. He gave us a lecture about paying the rent on time and maintaining the house and appliances.

During the fall semester, my housemates and I threw a party. We sent invitations to many friends and told everyone to come to our house on Friday night. We drew a large crowd and everyone had a great time. The last guests left in the wee[1] hours of the morning.

Exhausted, we decided to sleep in and clean the house and yard the next morning. Well, you guessed it! We were awakened about 7:00 a.m. by our landlord, who was knocking on the door. Sheepishly, we let him in, expecting to incur his wrath[2]. Instead, he picked up a party invitation that had been laying on the sidewalk and asked, "Why didn't you girls invite me?" He came into the house, made a minor repair, and spent a few minutes helping us pick up trash from the yard. We weren't quite sure what to make of our unexpected luck, but we were thrilled that our landlord had been so understanding.

A few months later, I made a mathematical error while balancing my checkbook and my bank soon notified me that I had bounced a check[3]. I was mortified[4] when I discovered that it was my rent check and that I had to notify my landlord. I figured that he viewed my housemates and I as irresponsible after the party

我们的好房东

大三的时候，我和两个朋友从衣阿华州立大学搬出来住。我们真的有点儿害怕我们的房东，他是一个有着粗鲁性格的中年人。他对我们说：要及时交月租，要完整保存好房子和配套的家用电器。

一个秋季的学期，我和我的室友举行了一次聚会，我们给许多朋友都发了请柬，告诉他们星期五晚上来聚会。那一天，我们一大群人玩得非常高兴。最后一个客人是在黎明前的几小时离开的。

我们简直是精疲力竭了，没有时间清理房屋，因此，我们先睡了，决定明天再打扫房子和庭院。然而，你猜猜！早上7点，我们就被房东的敲门声吵醒。睡眼惺忪的我们，让他进了屋，以为会招致他的怒气。相反，他却捡起地上的宴会请柬，问道："你们这些孩子为什么不邀请我？"他进了屋，简单的整理了一下屋子，并花了几分钟清理院子里的垃圾，我们也搞不懂为什么今天我们这么幸运，但是我们非常兴奋我们的房东竟变得这么能够理解人。

几个月后，由于我的疏忽，我的账户上没有余额了，银行给我发了退票。当我发现那是我给房东开的月租金的租赁支票时，我简直羞愧万分，于是我不得不通知我的房东。

❶ **wee**
/wiː/
adj. 很小的
❷ **wrath**
/ræθ/
n. 愤怒，暴怒
❸ **bounce a check**
（账户无钱）遭到银行退票
❹ **mortified**
/ˈmɔːtɪfaɪd/
adj. 羞愧的

incident and this would prove him right. I was certain that he would evict[5] me. Somehow, I mustered[6] the courage to call him and explained what had happened. He said, "I have a daughter about your age, and the same thing happened to her once. Would you like to wait until next month and send a double payment then?"

I've never forgotten our landlord's kindness and understanding. He also taught me an important lesson about not judging a book by its cover. I'm proud to say that I have not bounced[7] a check since (though I have thrown a few more parties)!

我猜那次聚会后他一定觉得我和我的室友是一群不负责任的人，而这一次的空头支票一定会再次验证他的想法，我觉得他一定会把我赶出去的。但是，我还是鼓起勇气给他打了个电话，向他解释发生的一切。他说："我的女儿和你们年龄相仿，她也做过类似的事。下个月，你给我两份租金不就成了吗？"

我真的无法忘记房东的和蔼和他的善解人意。他给我上了极为重要的一课，那就是不要从书皮去鉴定一本书的好坏（人不可貌相）！这里，我自豪地说，从那以后，银行再没给我发过退票（虽然我又举行了若干次聚会）。

❺ **evict**
/ɪˈvɪkt/
v. 逐出

❻ **muster**
/ˈmʌstə/
v. 召集；鼓起（勇气等）

❼ **bounce**
/ˈbaʊns/
v. 弹回

A learning experience
学习的体会

By learning about others, I learned more about myself and what I can do. I gained more confidence when I realized I could survive in the real world.

通过了解他人,我更加了解了自己,也明白了我所能做的是些什么。当我意识到我有生存能力时,我变得更加自信了。

情感篇

Over the last summer I volunteered at a summer camp for children aged 5 through 12. Every day for six weeks I used pedal[1] power to conquer the hill known only as Depot. Once I arrived at Abbot School at 7:30, I began my seven-hour day of cleaning, entertaining and giving piggyback[2] rides to a plethora[3] of small individuals, each with different plans of action and each needing his own special attention. By helping these kids and working with other counselors, I was able to develop a better sense of responsibility not just for myself, but for those around me.

In the beginning I helped with a group of twelve-year-olds. I had a lot of fun because they were the most mature campers, and I could relate to them. They didn't need as much help as the younger kids so the director of the camp switched me down to six-year-olds.

For the previous few years I had gone to an adventure camp in the woods of Maine. There I participated in rafting[4], rock-climbing, and sea-kayaking. But nothing, and I mean nothing, could have prevented from doing such kinds of adventures for a 15-year-old.

For the first summer I was doing something that benefited someone else, and I found more satisfaction in that than any wasted breezy day of summers past.

During this unique opportunity of giving a small part of my summer, I was able to get back so much more. I learned how

学习的体会

去年夏天，我志愿担任了5-12岁孩子的夏令营辅导员工作。夏令营为期6周，每天我都要骑车翻过那个名为Depot的山。每天7:30一到Abbot学校，我就开始了一天7个小时的繁重工作：清理打扫、陪小朋友玩耍、背着年龄很小的小朋友玩。他们每个人都有自己的行动计划，每个人都需要特殊的关照。通过帮助这些小朋友，通过与其他人一起工作，我养成了一种良好的责任感，不仅是对自己的责任感，更重要的是对他人的责任感。

开始的时候，我帮助的对象是一组12岁的孩子，和他们在一起我感到很愉快。他们是夏令营成员中年龄最大的，我们之间有一些共通之处。和那些年龄较小的孩子不同，他们不需要过多的帮助，因此，我被调往6岁的孩子组去帮忙。

前几年，我参加了缅因州森林的"冒险夏令营"活动。在那儿，我乘竹筏、攀岩、冲浪。那时，没有什么东西可以阻止一个15岁孩子去做那些事。

第一次，做了一些对他人有益的事情。我发现，那个夏日比其他任何一个轻风和畅被我荒废掉的夏日更让我满意。

这是一次把我暑期部分时间用在有意义事情上的难得机会，从中我收获很大：我学

❶ **pedal**
/ˈpedl/
adj. 脚踏的

❷ **piggyback**
/ˈpɪɡɪbæk/
adj. 骑在背肩上的

❸ **plethora**
/ˈpleθərə/
adj. 过多的

❹ **raft**
/rɑːft/
v. 乘筏，筏运

much my time is really worth and how to take responsibility for myself and especially others. I learned how different each individual is and how needs vary[5]. By learning about others, I learned more about myself and what I can do. I gained more confidence[6] when I realized I could survive in the real world.

会了我有多少时间是有意义的，又学会了如何对自己尤其是对他人负责，知道了每个个体都是那么不同，他们的需求变化又是那么大。通过了解他人，我更加了解了自己，也明白了我所能做的是些什么。当我意识到我有生存能力时，我变得更加自信了。

❺ **vary**
/ˈveərɪ/
v. 变化

❻ **confidence**
/ˈkɒnfɪdəns/
n. 自信

The last relationship
分 手

I always remember on a Sunday night you surprised me and said, "I LOVE YOU."
I replied to you and said, "I love you too always."

那个星期天的晚上让我铭记终身。你对我说:"我爱你。"
我对你答道:"我爱你一辈子!"

I remember the first time we met; you were as cute as can be and then we started to play fight then you sat on me.

You started to throw popcorn[1] while I was going down the stairs and I came back to beat[2] you up while you laid there.

I saw you again on Valentine's Day when I was a little shy, and didn't know what to say.

I remember the first time I asked you to come to my house with your brother; at first you didn't want to because of my mother, father, and brother.

When you came upstairs I was playing wit vane[3], I was hoping you were thinking — can I play with her?

While you were sitting on my couch changing channels on my TV, I was staring at[4] you hoping you wouldn't catch me.

Then we became all cool and started to play fight, you bit me and I bit you, and then we held each other a little tight.

Then I remember our first kiss; you were sitting on the chair I was in front of you and stood there.

But the moment had to last and you had to go and in my mind I was saying, "No, he can't go!"

分 手

记得我们初次相遇的情景,你是那么可爱。我们一起玩打仗,之后你骑在了我身上。

看到我从楼梯走下,你开始扔着爆米花,后来你躺在地上,我转身回去打了你。

再次见到你是在情人节的那天,我害羞得不知说什么。

记得第一次我邀请你和你的弟弟来我家做客,你不愿来,因为怕见我的父母和弟弟。

你上楼时,我正在玩风信旗。我真希望你是这样想的:我能和她一起玩风信旗吧?

你坐在沙发上,调换着电视频道,我款款深情地望着你,却希望不要碰到你的目光。

然后,我们冷静下来一起嬉戏打仗,你打我一下,我打你一下,我们彼此的心在慢慢靠近。

记得我们初吻的情景,你坐在椅子上,我站在你面前。

但是,时间无法停驻,你要走了,我在心里默念道:"别,不要走。"

❶ **popcorn**
/ˈpɒpkɔːn/
n. 爆米花

❷ **beat**
/biːt/
v. 打,跳动

❸ **vane**
/veɪn/
n. 风信旗

❹ **stare at**
盯着

Then on March the 3rd you asked me to be your girl and I replied yes and we became a couple; I was hoping there would be no trouble.

I always remember on a Sunday night you surprised me and said, "I LOVE YOU." I asked you over and over and said don't play. I replied to you and said, "I love you too always."

Then two months past, you said you wanted to leave so I said don't worry just stay calm. So later on, we were going our way, but sometimes we had our bad days.

It was about our 4th month we had planned a day so we went out, but we had a big argument and didn't know what to say.

Then the date finally came. You called me a bitch[5], so I got up and walked away. I walked away and stood behind a wall then I just thought "God please don't let this relationship fall."

As a tear dropped from my eye, you walked by and said, "Baby I'm sorry, please don't cry."

So finally we went home and you kissed me and I told you to go.

分 手

❺ bitch
/bɪtʃ/
n. 泼妇

然后，3月3日那天，你请求我要我成为你的女朋友，我答应了你，很快我们成为出双入对的情侣。我希望我们的感情从此能一帆风顺。

那个星期天的晚上让我铭记终身。你对我说："我爱你。"我问了你千万次，并对你说不要和我开玩笑。最后我对你答道："我爱你一辈子！"

两个月后，你说你想离开。我对你说不要这样，你需要冷静。之后，我们又在一起了，但是我们会常常发生一些小口角，那些日子过得不大愉快。

第四个月的某一天，我们计划一起出去，但也就是那一天，我们吵得很严重，彼此都不想说话。

那一天终于来临了。你骂我泼妇，我气愤地站起来转头走开。我站在一面墙后，祈祷："上帝呀，不要让我们的关系破裂。"

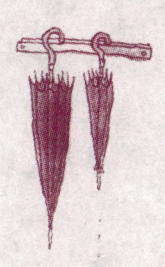

我的眼泪慢慢滑下，你走过来对我说，"宝贝，我错了，别哭了！"

You made new friends and went out and do you know I sat there pissed[6], mad, and a kind of blue.

So then I finally told you, you don't need me and I don't need you.

So you said let's just take a break 1 month, 2 months then I felt like it went away.

Then after a while you called me that you miss me, you love me and you want me.

We talked for a while, I was being cold then you asked me again and I explained my self and then said no.

So after that I wrote about a guy who stole my heart away as we said goodbye, he went his way and I went mine and here I am today.

分　手

最终，我俩一起回到家中，你亲吻了我，我对你下了逐客令。

❻ pissed
/pɪst/
adj. 恼火的

你交了新朋友，并与她们一起出去玩，可你不知道我有多生气，我有多恼怒，我有多伤心。

于是我对你说我们彼此不再需要对方了。

你只是说让我们先分开一个月吧，可我觉得像是过去了两个月那么久。

一段时间后，你打电话对我说你爱我，想念我，想让我回到你身边。

我态度冰冷地和你聊了一会儿，你又让我回到你身边，我解释说一切都不再可能了。

此后，我写道，就是这个我与之分手的男孩偷走了我的心。我们分道扬镳，他走他的路，我走我的路。如今，我仍旧好好地在这儿生活着。

Life is a gift
生活本身就是一种礼物

Life is a gift,
Enjoy it...
Celebrate it...
And fulfill it.

生活是一份礼物，
享受它……
庆祝它……
实现它。

情感篇

Today before you think of saying an unkind word,
Think of someone who can't speak.

Before you complain[1] about the taste of your food,
Think of someone who has nothing to eat.

Before you complain about your husband or wife,
Think of someone who's crying out to God for a companion[2].

Today before you complain about life,
Think of someone who went too early to heaven.

Before you complain about your children,
Think of someone who desires children but they're barren.

Before you <u>argue about</u>[3] your dirty house someone didn't clean or sweep,
Think of the people who are living in the streets.

Before whining[4] about the distance you drive,
Think of someone who walks the same distance with their feet.

And when you are tired and complain about your job,
Think of the unemployed, the disabled and those who wished they had your job.

现在，就在你出言不逊前，
想想吧，还有一些人不能开口说话。

在你抱怨食物不够鲜美前，
想想吧，有一些人还在忍饥挨饿。

在抱怨丈夫不够体贴或妻子不够温顺前，
想想吧，还有一些人正在发愁没有伴侣。

现在，就在你对生活表示不满前，
想想吧，有些人已经早早地去了天国。

在抱怨你的孩子不够听话前，
想想吧，有些人因为没有子嗣而正在渴求孩子。

在抱怨你的房子没人清理、打扫前，
想想吧，一些人身无居所，睡在大街上。

在抱怨趟车所要行驶的遥远路途前，
想想吧，有些人步行着同样的距离。

在你感到疲惫、抱怨工作前，
想想那些下岗工人，想想那些残疾人，
想想那些渴求有你这样一份工作的人吧。

❶ complain
/kəmˈpleɪn/
v. 抱怨

❷ companion
/kəmˈpænjən/
n. 伴侣，同伴

❸ argue about
争吵

❹ whine
/waɪn/
v. 抱怨

But before you think of pointing the finger or condemning[5] another,

Remember that not one of us are without sin and we all answer to one maker.

And when depressing thoughts seem to get you down,
Put a smile on your face and thank God you're alive and still around.

Life is a gift,
Enjoy it...
Celebrate it...
And fulfill[6] it.

And while you want to give love to someone today,
Love someone with what you do and the words you say,
Love is not meant to be kept locked inside of us and hidden,
So give it away "Give Love to someone today!"

在指责别人前，
记住吧，我们所有人都有罪孽，而且我们都向一个造物主尽我们的责任。

当悲观想法使你沮丧、失意时，
绽放一个微笑吧，感谢上帝赐予你生命吧。

生活是一份礼物，
享受它……
庆祝它……
实现它。

今天你要向别人表示爱，
用你的言行去爱吧，
爱情不应封藏在心中，
表示出来吧，"爱在今天！"

❺ **condemn**
/kən'dem/
v. 谴责

❻ **fulfill**
/fʊl'fɪl/
v. 达到，履行

Two interesting jokes
笑话二则

"Oh", she said, "I'm so glad you called. I remembered saying 'yes' to someone, but I couldn't remember who it was."

她说道:"噢,非常高兴你给我打电话,我只知道我答应了某人的求婚,但记不得答应谁了"。

Marriage Proposal

An elderly widow[1] and widower[2] have been dating for about five years. The man finally decided to ask her to marry. She immediately said "yes". The next morning when he awoke, he couldn't remember what her answer was! "Was she happy? I think so, wait, no, she looked at me funny..." After about an hour of trying to remember to no avail[3] he got on the telephone and gave her a call. Embarrassed[4], he admitted that he didn't remember her answer to the marriage proposal[5]. "Oh", she said, "I'm so glad you called. I remembered saying 'yes' to someone, but I couldn't remember who it was."

The Elevator

A boy and his father were visiting a mall. They were amazed by almost everything they saw, but especially by two shiny, silver walls that could move apart and back together again. The boy asked his father, "What is this, Father?" The father — never having seen an elevator — responded "Son, I have never seen anything like this in my life, I don't know what it is."

While the boy and his father were watching wide-eyed, an old lady in a wheel chair rolled up to the moving walls and pressed a button. The walls opened and the lady rolled between them into a small room. The walls closed and the boy and his fa-

求 婚

一对上了年纪的寡妇和鳏夫约会了5年。最后，这个男人向这位寡妇求婚，她立刻答道"好吧"。第二天醒来，他记不起那位寡妇回答什么了。"她高兴吗？我觉得她很高兴。不，等等，她看我的表情很可笑……"想了一个小时，他还是记不得她的答案。因此，他给她拨了个电话，他尴尬地承认自己记不得她是怎样回答他的求婚的。她说道："噢，非常高兴你给我打电话，我只知道我答应了某人的求婚，但记不得答应谁了"。

❶ **widow**
/ˈwɪdəʊ/
n. 寡妇

❷ **widower**
/ˈwɪdəʊə/
n. 鳏夫

❸ **avail**
/əˈveɪl/
v. 利用，有用

❹ **embarrassed**
/ɪmˈbærəst/
adj. 尴尬的

❺ **proposal**
/prəˈpəʊzəl/
n. 求婚

电 梯

一个孩子和父亲来城里的购物中心，他们惊叹自己见到的一切，尤其是那两面亮晶晶、银闪闪，可开可合的墙。儿子问父亲："这是什么，爸爸？"父亲（从未见过电梯）回答道："儿子，我从未见过这个东西，我也不知道它是什么。"

儿子和父亲睁大双眼盯着这面墙。这时，一个坐在轮椅上的老太太手摇轮椅来到一直运动的墙前，按了一个按钮，墙开了，老太

ther watched small circles of lights with numbers above the walls light up. They continued to watch the circles light up in the reverse[6] direction.

The walls opened up again and a beautiful 24-year-old woman stepped out. The father said to his son, "Go get your mother."

太进到一个小房子里,墙又合上了。父亲和儿子盯着墙上方闪着数字的小圈灯闪过去又闪回来。

　　墙又开了,一个 24 岁的漂亮女人出来了。父亲对儿子说:"快去叫你妈去。"

6 reverse
/rɪˈvɜːs/
adj. 相反的

A father and a son
父亲和儿子

The father and son, though, were just riding this shuttle together, making it exciting, sharing each other's company.

尽管这位父亲和他的儿子只是在乘坐巴士火车,但是他们彼此陪伴,使他们的行程异常精彩。

Passing through the Atlanta airport one morning, I caught one of those trains that take travelers from the main terminal[1] to their boarding gates. Free, sterile and impersonal[2], the trains run back and forth all day long. Not many people consider them fun, but on this Saturday I heard laughter.

At the front of the first car-looking out the window at the track that lay ahead, were a man and his son. They had just stopped to let off passengers, and the doors were closing again. "Here we go! Hold on to me tight! " the father said. The boy, about five years old, made sounds of sheer[3] delight.

I know we're supposed to avoid making racial distinctions these days, so I hope no one will mind if I mention that most people on the train were white, dressed for business trips or vacations — and that the father and son were black, dressed in clothes that were just about as inexpensive as you can buy.

"Look out there," the father said to his son. "See that pilot? I bet he's walking to his plane." The son craned his neck to look[4].

As I got off, I remembered something I'd wanted to buy in the terminal. I was early for my flight, so I decided to go back.

I did and just as I was about to re-board the train for my gate, I saw that the man and his son had returned too. I realized then that they hadn't been heading for a flight, but had just been riding the shuttle.

父亲和儿子

一天早上，经过亚特兰大机场，我看到了把旅游者从终点站带到登机入口的巴士火车，每天，它们都机械地往返于两地之间。并不是许多人都觉得这些火车有趣，但在这个星期六，我却听到了从火车上传来的笑声。

第一节车厢里，坐着一位男士和他的儿子，此时他们正探出窗外去看火车的轨道，火车停下了来，乘客陆续下了车。车门又一次关上，"走这边！抓紧我！"父亲这样说道。这个大约5岁的小男孩，发出了欢快的叫声。

我知道在今天这个年代，我们不应该再存有种族区分，所以当我提到以下种种描述时，希望各位不要介意。这辆火车上大多数是白人，他们穿着赶赴商务之行或去度假的那种名贵服装；然而，这位父亲和他的儿子却是黑人，穿着那种人人买得起的便宜服装。

"看那儿，"父亲对儿子说，"看到那个飞行员了吗？我猜他一定去他的飞机。"儿子伸长脖子去看那位飞行员。

下车后，我记起要在车站买一些东西，由于到机场很早，我决定返回去买。

正当我再次上火车想返回车站时，我看到那个父亲和他的儿子也回来搭乘火车。此时，我意识到他们并不是去坐飞机，而是一直在乘往返两地的巴士火车。

❶ terminal
/ˈtɜːmɪnəl/
n. 终点站

❷ impersonal
/ɪmˈpɜːsənəl/
adj. 冷淡的，没有人情的

❸ sheer
/ʃɪə/
adj. 彻底的，十足的

❹ crane one's neck to look
伸长脖子看

"You want to go home now? " the father asked.

"I want to ride some more! "

"More? " the father said, mocking exasperation[5] but clearly pleased. "You're not tired? "

"This is fun!! " his son said.

"All right," the father replied, and when a door opened we all got on.

There are parents who can afford to send their children to Europe or Disneyland, and the children turn out rotten. There are parents who live in million-dollar houses and give their children cars and swimming pools, yet something goes wrong.

"Where are all these people going, Daddy? " the son asked.

"All over the world," came the reply. The other people in the airport were leaving for distant destinations or arriving at the ends of their journeys. The father and son, though, were just riding this shuttle together, making it exciting, sharing each other's company[6].

He was a father who cared about spending the day with his son and who had come up with[7] this plan on a Saturday morning.

"想回家吗?"父亲问道。
"我想再坐几次。"

"再坐几次?"父亲问道,他假装恼火但明显很高兴。"你不累吗?"
"这太有趣了!!"儿子答道。

"好吧!"父亲答道。此时门开了,我们都上了车。

世界上有这样的父母,他们可以支付得起孩子到欧洲或迪斯尼乐园的旅游费用,然而他们的孩子最后堕落了。也有这样一些父母,他们拥有千万资产,可以给他们的孩子买汽车和华贵的游泳池,然而这些孩子却变坏了。

"爸爸,那些人去哪儿呢?"儿子问道。

"世界各地,"他答道。飞机场上的乘客将要前往遥远的目的地,有的将要抵达旅行的终点站。尽管这位父亲和他的儿子只是在乘坐巴士火车,但是他们彼此陪伴,使他们的行程异常精彩。

这位父亲愿意在星期六的早上提出这样一种出行计划,愿意花一天的时间来陪儿子。

❺ exasperation
/ɪɡˌzæspəˈreɪʃən/
n. 恼怒
❻ company
/ˈkʌmpəni/
n. 陪同
❼ come up with
计划或提出某物

Parents who care enough to spend time, and to pay attention and to try their best. It doesn't cost a cent, yet it is the most valuable[8] thing in the world.

The train picked up speed, and the father pointed something out, and the boy laughed again.

一些父母愿意花时间、花精力，并尽最大的努力去关心他的孩子，所有这些都不会花掉一分一厘的钱，但是这种行为本身却是世界上最珍贵的东西。

火车开得更快了，那位父亲还在给儿子指着什么，孩子又笑了起来。

❽ **valuable**
/ˈvæljuəbl/
adj. 珍贵的

Speed skater tells story with heart and emotion
短道速滑手充满深情的故事

If it's possible to feel your soul being touched then that is what I felt.

如果灵魂能够被触摸,那么当时我就有一种灵魂被触摸的感觉。

情 感 篇

In his autobiography[1], "Reflections in the Ice," Olympic Gold Medal winning speed skater Derek Parra remembers being asked by the U.S. Olympic Committee "to carry the world Trade Center American Flag into the Opening Ceremonies of the 2002 Olympic Winter Games. They had selected eight athletes from the American team for this honor and I was one of them. I was floored!"

He knew "instantly" he should do it, even though he had planned on skipping opening ceremonies so he could stay off his feet and be at his best for his race the next morning. "It was an honor beyond anything I could have imagined. I immediately called my wife, Tiffany, and she agreed completely. I discussed it with my coach (Bart) and agent (Pat). Each ... recognized the magnitude[2] of the moment. . . . When it came time to begin the procession, I touched the flag for the first time and felt a physical sensation unlike anything I had ever experienced. If it's possible to feel your soul being touched then that is what I felt."

Even as[3] Parra was strongly identifying with those who died on 9/11, he was unwittingly[4] awaiting the climax to his arduous[5] physical training when he would win two events at Salt Lake City, garnering[6] both a silver and a gold medal. The next 17 days, he says, were "the most remarkable" of his life.

Parra, who has given numerous speeches, especially to young people, since his victory, attempts to portray the feelings in his heart that allowed "a short Mexican kid" to reach his athletic

短道速滑手充满深情的故事

奥运会短道速滑金牌获得者 Derek Parra 在他的自传《冰上回忆》中写道，美国奥运会组委会曾经委任他一项坚巨的任务，"他们把在 2002 年冬奥会开幕式上，举世贸大厦上的美国国旗的任务交给了我。他们一共选了八名美国运动员，我是其中的一位，我当时真的有点犯难！"

但是，他立刻意识到他应该接下这个任务，尽管他确实不想参加冬奥会的开幕典礼，因为这样可以得到充分休息以便调整到最佳状态进行第二天的比赛。"我从没奢想过如此的殊荣。我立刻给我的妻子 Tiffany 通了个电话，她完全赞成我接下这个任务。我和我的教练（Bart）以及我的经纪人（Pat）都进了商讨，他们每个人都承认这是一件非比寻常的重要大事。列队前进的时刻终于到来了，第一次我触摸到了美国国旗，那一刻一种从未有过的激动包围着我。如果灵魂能够被触摸，那么当时我就有一种灵魂被触摸的感觉。"

当 Parra 还在对 9·11 事件遇难者表示深深同情时，没人预料到在盐湖城的冬奥会上，他迎来了自己事业的巅峰，那次大赛里，他获得一金一银。他说道："接下来的 17 天是我生命中最辉煌的时刻。"

Parra 做过许多演讲报告，尤其是给年轻

❶ **autobiography**
/ˌɔːtəbaɪˈɒɡrəfɪ/
n. 自传

❷ **magnitude**
/ˈmæɡnɪtjuːd/
n. 重要性

❸ **even as**
正当，恰恰

❹ **unwittingly**
/ʌnˈwɪtɪŋlɪ/
adv. 不知不觉地，不知道地

❺ **arduous**
/ˈɑːdjʊəs/
adj. 艰巨的

❻ **garner**
/ˈɡɑːnə/
v. 收集并贮藏某物

pinnacle. With emotion, he describes his broken home life, one-hundred-mile bike rides, eating McDonald's trash and the serious formation of goals. Before leaving his teens, Parra became a determined young man who believed life's dreams could be fulfilled.

He describes picking roller skating as the sport to excel in[7], beginning at the age of 14, followed by intensive training, opportunities to compete all over the world, receiving accolades and prizes and still believing there was something else he should do. So he switched from online skating to ice skating when he was 26 and went on to Olympic glory.

Although the book contains a lot of tired quotations taken from self-help books, Parra's personal story is compelling[8]. Young people are likely to find inspiration here to stoke the fires of their own lives.

He is touching when he talks of Tiffany, now that he is a father of their first child, he feels more connected to family than he ever did in his own difficult, growing years. For those who are cynical[9] about athletes who sell themselves as role models for youth, Parra seems a breath of fresh air.

人。他的成功向我们刻画了他内心的思想和感情，那就是"一个瘦小的墨西哥孩子"达到了自己体育竞技的顶峰。他充满深情地向我们讲述了他破碎的家庭生活，每天骑车跋涉100英里的艰苦情景，吃麦当劳垃圾食品，以及他心中的宏伟目标。20岁的时候，Parra成长为一名意志坚定的有志青年，他始终认为心中的理想一定会有实现的那一天。

他在书中写道，他14岁时，早冰就已滑得很出色。之后，他受过一段时间大强度的集中训练，终于迎来了与世界各级选手竞赛的机会，那次他获得了奖项，受到了肯定。但是，他认为他还可以向其他领域扩展。因此，26岁时，他开始从事真正的滑冰，并且向奥运会进军。

尽管他的书中有许多源于自助书籍的陈旧引文，但是Parra的亲身故事依旧是那么的引人入胜。年轻人一定会从中受到许多启发和鼓励，并点燃对生活的热情。

谈到妻子Tiffany，他非常动情，他现在已经是一个孩子的父亲了，和那时艰苦的成长岁月对比，他现在更注重家庭。有些运动员玩世不恭、标榜自己是年轻人的楷模，但是，Parra却不同，他就像一缕清新的空气。

❼ **excel in**
擅长某物
❽ **compelling**
/kəmˈpelɪŋ/
adj. 引人入胜的
❾ **cynical**
/ˈsɪnɪkəl/
adj. 愤世嫉俗的

My one and only
我的惟一

I used to say that I hate him but later on ... I only eat my words.

我常说我痛恨他，但是后来……我食言了。

情感篇

It was all started when I was in high school; I still remember my love one. I am not sure if it is puppy love[1] or first love, but I know deep inside my heart that I still remember him.

At first we were bus mate, and schoolmate too. I was in 1st year high school and he was in second. We still don't know each other before, but later on when I was sitting in front of him in the bus, he used to talk and tease me, which makes me angry with him. I used to say that I hate him but later on .... I only eat my words. One day when my best friends wanted to see what I wrote in my diary, I was reading it in the bus and without noticing the guy whom I hate was sitting back of me with his buddies[2]. He was peeping[3] and reading the things what I wrote in the diary. I looked sharply at him and put the book down, then my friend who was in front of me that she has read what I wrote there that love is BOG, BOG, BOG in my heart. He was hearing it and suddenly without my knowledge he stood and snatched the diary from me! Whew! What he did was to read the book so loudly where everything was written there about love! Goodness! I was so shocked that I was screaming[4] just to get it back. I couldn't believe it, because he's the most intelligent student in my school and he's the representative of our school too. Then after the bus dropped me to my house there I felt that I was so flushing hotly that my cheeks were so red! There, I realized that I have a crush on him[5]!

Sports date came, and he was the champion for C group boys for running. Whew! Wow! I was really amazed when he runs, because he always come 1st in running and he runs like a

所有的一切都始于我的高中时代，直到现在我仍记得他，我不能确定那是孩子间不成熟的恋情，还是我的初恋，但我知道在我的内心深处，我始终无法忘却他。

一开始，我们只是同学、路友。我上高一，他上高二，之前，我们互不相识。但是，后来，在公共汽车上，我坐在他的前面，他经常拿话题取笑我，这使我极为恼怒。我常说我痛恨他，但是后来我食言了。一天，我的好朋友想看看我平时都写了些什么，我在汽车上读起来我本子上写的东西。当然，我不知道我非常痛恨的那个男孩和他的一群兄弟就坐在我的后面。他偷看我写的内容，当时，我用犀利地眼神看着他，赶快把本子放下。这时，坐在我前面的好朋友对我说她读完我写的东西，她说在我心中我把爱情比作"泥潭"。那个男孩听到这些话，突然站起身来把我的本子抢走了。天呀，他大声地朗读着我所写的内容，本子上写的内容全都是关于爱情的！我尖叫着把我的东西抢回来，我真的不敢相信这就是全校最聪明的学生，这就是我们学校的学生代表。汽车停下后，我赶忙奔到家中，我害羞地直发热，脸颊也变得通红！那时我意识到我有些喜欢他。

体育竞赛的时刻到来了，他获得了C组

❶ puppy love
未成人男女不成熟的爱情

❷ buddy
/ˈbʌdl/
n. 老兄，伙伴

❸ peep
/piːp/
v. 偷看，窥视

❹ scream
/skriːm/
v. 喊叫，尖叫

❺ have a crush on sb.
迷恋，喜欢某人

wind. That day I felt more feelings for him. I used to write him always in my diary, but mostly he always went to another place because of interschool quiz.

I cried that time, because I was missing him so much, that I wish one day he'll like me too. Then one day I just heard that he likes me! My god, I nearly faint! Rumors spread that in the bus we always fights for simple things like teasing, because I use to call him NUTCRACKER[6] which makes him so mad at me, and I always teased him for his pimples[7] and about his using FACIAL cleanser which made my whole bus mates burst out laughing, and he was blushing, and then one fine day the rumors spread that we both are loving each other! Whenever we cross our paths we just look each other casually, but my hearts beats fast because he looks at me so intensely[8] which makes my heart tremble. I used to be always so naughty that time. One day I decided to ask my friend to write a love letter in language of German I loved, since we both are different nation.

My friend wrote it, and in the bus I asked him to read the letter for me. He read it and explained what was written, and I know the last word written there was just I love you, but he told me that the last word means "I love you" which makes me blushed! Oh even though I know that he wasn't the one who wrote it, but it seems like he is telling it from his heart!

But not all the love story has happy ending ...

男生的冠军！他经常赢得跑步冠军，我很惊叹他的跑步速度，犹如风一样快。那天，我对他又多了一些感觉，我还会常在日记里写到他。但他经常不在学校，因为他经常参加一些校际竞赛。

有一次，因为太想念他，我哭了起来，我真的希望有那么一天他会喜欢我。一天，当我听别人说他喜欢我时，我几乎晕过去了。以前，大家常说我俩总为一些小事，比如相互讥讽而在汽车上大动干戈。我常常叫他"坚果钳"，这使他气愤不已，我常常取笑他因为脸上的粉刺而用洗面奶，这使得全车的人听后都捧腹大笑，他简直就是羞红了脸。突然有一天，却传出我们彼此喜欢对方！不论什么时候穿过街头，我们也只是偶尔地相互看看。我的心在他热烈的目光下跳得很快，而且开始颤抖。那时，我很调皮，有一天，我决定让我的朋友用我喜欢的德语写一封情书，因为，我们俩不是来自一个国家。我的朋友写好了这封情书了。在车上，我让他给我念，他边读边给我解释情书的内容，我知道情书上最后写的是"我爱你"。他念到那儿时，告诉我，那几个字的意思是"我爱你"。这句话使我的脸颊绯红，即使我知道这不是他写的，但这仿佛是他的心声。

❻ **nutcracker**
/ˈnʌtˌkrækə/
n. 坚果钳

❼ **pimple**
/ˈpɪmpl/
n. 粉刺

❽ **intensely**
/ɪnˈtensli/
adv. 激情地,强烈地

One day, I heard that he likes another girl which makes my heart break! In the bus, I used to make him jealous of me by saying that I have a boy friend. I made it, and he was jealous! Then examination came. I was really broken-heart when I saw him waiting for a girl in the gate! I cried, because of his caring for dating girl. Five days before the exam came, he told me in the bus that he's going to his country! My god! I can't believe it. He's leaving me! The last day in the school and in the bus, I took a picture of him in my own camera! And when he went down in the bus I told bye ... and then I still can't believe that he's gone.

To tell you we both are in the same bus, same school, we both are born on the same year. That was HAMLET! By Shakespeare I was the dancer, and he's Hamlet. I can never forget my one, my only one. He dreamed about me so many times! He even include the poem A KISS IN THE RAIN in his dream and we both composed[9] a poem for each other, I composed a poem for him "ONLY YOU", and he composed a poem for me "SHE'S MINE". I still can't forget the happy unforgettable moments once we shared! Oh, nostalgia[10] —

但是，并不是每个爱情故事都有幸福的结尾。

一天，听别人说，他喜欢了别的女孩，我的心都快碎了。在车上，我故意和别人说我已经有男朋友了，故意让他嫉妒，他真的是极为嫉妒。考试的日子来临了，我看到他在门口正等着和一个女孩约会。我哭了，因为他开始在意别的女孩了。考试前的五天，在车上，他告诉我他要回国了，我几乎不相信自己的耳朵。最后一天，在校园里、在车上，我用自己的相机给他拍了好多照片。他乘上了回国的汽车，我向他摆手道别，我不敢相信，他离开了我。

告诉你们，我们以前坐同一班汽车，我们在同一所学校读书，我们同年出生，简直就是莎士比亚笔下的《哈姆雷特》，我便是那个舞女，他就是哈姆雷特。我永远无法忘记他，他也常常在梦里梦到我，他甚至编了一首诗《雨中吻》。我们彼此都给对方写着情诗，我为他写下《只有你》这首诗，他为我写下了《她是我的》这首诗。无法忘记我们一起走过的那些高兴的、令人难忘的时光！怀旧的思绪呀……

❾ compose
/kəm'pəʊz/
v. 创作，构成

❿ nostalgia
/nɒ'stældʒɪə/
n. 怀旧，乡愁

An unforgettable Christmas
令人难忘的圣诞节

At the sight of my brothers, I screamed, and I started crying; I had NO idea they were coming!

看到两个哥哥,我激动地尖叫起来,喜极而泣。我一点儿也不知道他们要来。

I still can't believe what my husband has done for me.

He got me a CAR for Christmas; and I don't even know HOW to drive yet!

I woke up early Christmas morning, and after I took my medications[1], I went to the living room, only to see the Christmas tree all lit up and all the presents underneath[2]. I knew that "Santa Claus" had come, and I knew that the children would be all excited when they saw all the presents underneath the tree; and that was when I heard some loud laughter coming in from the kitchen. The kitchen light was on, and I slowly made my way to the kitchen, and much to my surprise, there was my husband, Roberto, chatting with MY BROTHERS, Keserian and Naiser! At the sight of my brothers, I screamed, and I started crying; I had NO idea they were coming! Keserian and Naiser both started crying when they saw me, and soon, we were hugging each other, and we were all crying from joy and excitement at seeing each other again!

I then heard the children from their rooms (Kibarake and Eshe were both crying sleepily, and Jubaki was yelling, "It's CHRISTMAS! It's CHRISTMAS! Did Santy come? Did Santy come??"), so I told Roberto to take care of the children while I visited with my brothers. I couldn't believe how well both Naiser and Keserian looked; and I was surprised at how well Keserian was getting around on forearm crutches[3] and leg braces. The last time I saw Keserian back in Kenya last summer, he was still in

我还是不能相信我丈夫为我做的一切。

圣诞节那天，他送给我一辆汽车，可是我几乎不知道怎么开车！

圣诞节的一大早我就起床了，吃完药后，刚走进起居室，便看到了光彩照人的圣诞树，树下堆满了圣诞礼物。我知道"圣诞"老人已经来了，我知道孩子们见到这些礼物一定会兴奋地大叫起来。这时，我听到从厨房传来响亮的笑声。厨房的灯亮着，我慢慢走向厨房，让我惊喜万分的是，我丈夫Roberto，正在与我的两个哥哥Keserian和Naiser闲聊。看到两个哥哥，我激动地尖叫起来，喜极而泣。我一点儿也不知道他们要来。两个哥哥见到我后，也激动地哭了起来，互相拥抱后，我们又一次因见到彼此而掉下幸福、激动的泪水。

我听到了孩子们从房间传出来的声音(Kibarake和Eshe嚷嚷着喊困，Jubaki叫嚷道："今天是圣诞节！今天是圣诞节！圣诞老人来了没有呀？")。我让Roberto去照看孩子，我留下和哥哥说话。我简直不敢相信自己的眼睛，Keserian和Naisern看起来气色很好。我很惊讶Keserian是如何克服困难运用自如地使用手中的拐杖和腿上的支架。最后一次见到他还是在去年夏天，那时他还在肯尼亚住院，根本不能走动，因为他当时正在

❶ medication
/ˌmedɪˈkeɪʃən/
n. 药物，药剂

❷ underneath
/ˌʌndəˈniːθ/
adv. 在底下，在下面

❸ crutch
/krʌtʃ/
n. 拐杖

hospital, and at the time he couldn't walk, as he was recovering from his injuries.

After the kids were up, washed up, and were dressed, Roberto then brought them into the livingroom, and Jubaki was yelling[4], "He CAME! Oh, Santy CAME!! He brought presents for Jubaki!!", and the twins were amazed at the sight of all the brightly wrapped presents under the lighted up Christmas tree. Roberto then started passing out presents after everyone was seated in the livingroom. The biggest cry came when Jubaki got his big gift, which, to my surprise, was a remote control[5] Hummer. The Hummer was yellow, and it came with batteries and a remote control, which could be operated by pushing a few buttons, and depending on which buttons you pressed, it could go forwards or backwards. I wasn't none too happy either when I found out that the toy remote-control Hummer cost $99.00 at Wal-Mart!

After the presents had all been opened, Roberto then handed me an envelope that had my name on it. When I opened it, there were a set of car keys in it, and nothing else. I looked at him all confused; but then I heard the noise of a car horn beeping, and Roberto quickly got up, and when he looked out the window, he grinned, and he said, "Honey, your present is here. Look out the front window, and you will see your Christmas present. It's from me." When I looked out, I nearly fainted. There, sitting in the driveway, was a beautiful orange Volkswagen Beetle that had a bright red Christmas bow wrapped around it and a

令人难忘的圣诞节

恢复伤口。

孩子们起床、洗漱穿衣完毕后，Roberto 把他们带到起居室，Jubaki 叫道："他来了，圣诞老人来了！他给 Jubaki 带礼物来了！"另外两个孪生小兄弟惊异地看着闪闪发光的圣诞树下那些包装精美的礼物。他们坐好后，Roberto 开始分发礼物。接到礼物后，Jubaki 发出了兴奋的大叫。令我惊异的是，那是一个遥控的电动狗，是一个配有电池和遥控器的黄颜色的电动狗。只要按一下遥控器上的按钮，就可以控制电动狗，电动狗会根据你按的不同的按钮或前或后移动。但是，当我发现这个玩具在沃尔玛超市卖 99 美元时，我稍有点儿不悦。

所有的礼物都打开后，Roberto 递给我一个上面写着我名字的信封。打开后，我发现除了一串车钥匙外，什么都没有。我困惑地看着他，这时我听到了"嘟——嘟——嘟"的汽车喇叭声。Roberto 马上站起来，望着窗外，咧嘴笑道："亲爱的，你的礼物在这儿。从前窗望出去，你就会看到我送给你的圣诞礼物。"我望后，差点儿晕倒。那儿，一辆非常漂亮的桔色大众甲壳虫停在路上，车上系着一条红色的圣诞标幅，上面写道："圣诞快乐！爱你的 Roberto。"看到这辆车，我禁不住哭了，我对

❹ **yell**
/yel/
v. 叫喊，叫嚷

❺ **remote control**
遥控器

sign on the front that said, "Merry Christmas! With love, your husband, Roberto". When I saw the car, I couldn't help but to start crying. I then said to him, "You got me a car??" and he said, "Yes! Merry Christmas, darling!"

Now it is two days after Christmas, and I still can't believe that my husband spent that kind of money on me! He doesn't need to be doing that, you know...he's got kids and a wife to take care of; he doesn't need to be spending all that extra money on me! Especially on stuff[6] like remote-control Hummers, let alone, a real life car!! Do you know that real Beetles cost at least $11,000?? They aren't cheap!! And he expects me to learn to drive that thing?? Oh——

他说:"你给我买车了?"他答道:"是的,亲爱的,圣诞快乐!"

圣诞节已经过去两天了,我还是不能相信我丈夫把那么多钱用在我身上。其实,他无需这样做。要知道他有妻子和孩子要养活,他真的不用为我花多余的钱,尤其这些电动狗,更别提那辆车了。要知道甲壳虫要1万1千美元呢,它非常贵。他还在期望着我学开那辆车呢,噢——

6 stuff
/stʌf/
n. 物品,东西

Dealing with anger
控制愤怒

If you find your honking your horn at traffic, if you are not able to concentrate on your work like you want to, these are all ways of knowing that something is wrong.

如果你发现自己在道路行车时按喇叭,或者不能像自己想要的那样集中精力工作,这些都能表示已经出了问题。

情 感 篇

Q: What causes[1] a person to experience anger?
A: There are basically two ways of experiencing anger. You can feel angry with yourself over not having done as well as you had hoped on an examination, or you can have the other kind of anger, which is directed at someone else, or some object. In other words, you can stub[2] your toe walking over a carpet and be angry with that, or you can be angry at a sales person in the store, or with a spouse[3] of girlfriend/boyfriend as a result of an argument or dispute. Internal anger is directed at yourself for something that you have done or not done and external anger is the result of an interaction with another person.

Q: What are some ways of dealing with anger?
A: Probably the most productive way is taking your angry feelings to the source, in other words, directly to the person involved. If your angry feeling are directed at yourself and you are angry with yourself about something, try to express those feelings to a friend, a colleague or a counselor. In other words, to kind of get it off[4] your chest. It is very important to get out angry feelings regardless of[5] what kind of anger you're feeling.

Q: What are some of the non-productive ways of dealing with anger?
A: Instead of expressing feelings, the non-productive way would be to bottle them up, keeping those feelings inside. An expression that is frequently used is "sandbagging". Sandbagging your angry feelings means to avoid the person, for whom anger is directed, sidestepping[6] the issue, keeping the anger inside, instead of being direct with a person. Sandbagging re-

问：什么会引发人们的怒火？

答：基本上有两种方式能够引起愤怒。如果考试没有达到你的预期，你会跟自己生气，或者你会对某人或某物生气，这是愤怒的另一种形式。换句话说，在地毯上走路戳到了脚趾，你会为此生气，你也可能在商店里对推销员生气，或者由于男女朋友、夫妻间的争吵而生气。内在的愤怒是由于你做了或没做某事而直接针对自己，外在的愤怒则是和他人互动的结果。

问：有什么办法能克服发火呢？

答：也许最有效的办法就是找到让你生气的根源，就是说直接找到让你生气的人。如果你是跟自己生气或者是由于某件事情生气，那么试着向你的朋友、同事、心理咨询师倾诉你的感受，让自己能够直抒胸臆。这对排解任何愤怒的情绪都很重要。

问：什么是控制愤怒的无效办法呢？

答：相对于倾诉感情，无效的方法就是把这些情绪都憋在心里。有一个词语经常被用来形容这种情况：心理壁垒。在你愤怒的感情周围筑起一道壁垒就意味着不直接面对让你生气的人，回避问题，把怒气藏在心

❶ cause
/kɔːz/
v. 引起，使造成

❷ stub
/stʌb/
v. (脚趾)碰到某物

❸ spouse
/spaʊz/
n. 配偶

❹ get sth. off
从某物上移去某物

❺ regardless of
不论

❻ sidestep
/ˈsaɪdstep/
v. 回避

sults in being indirect and sarcastic. Many people fear hurting someone else's feelings if they share angry feelings. Yet by holding on to anger, the other person ends up feeling hurt and relationships are damaged. Having a lot of angry feelings that are pent up could lead to punitive kinds of behavior or resentment, directly or indirectly. People that you are involved with, a boyfriend of girlfriend or a spouse, know when you are angry. There are ways that you show it indirectly. And when you don't express that anger directly to them, usually they resent it, and the frustration can cause people to withdraw from each other.

Q: Many people are not even aware they are angry, or that they're not expressing it. How does a person become aware of[7] whether they're expressing their anger or not?

A: One way for people to tell whether they are angry is if they are short tempered. If you find your honking[8] your horn at traffic, if you are not able to concentrate on your work like you want to, these are all ways of knowing that something is wrong. Agitated feelings are good clues to unexpressed anger. Also, there are occasionally some physical symptoms that go along with unexpressed anger, such as migraine headaches, peptic ulcers, upset stomach, tension headaches. Usually your body tells you that something is wrong. You are bottling something up, and you are not expressing those angers.

Q: Is there a decision-making process related to expressing anger?

A: When you have angry feelings, you have to decide if this is

里,不向他人倾诉。心理壁垒会导致虚伪和讽刺。很多人生气的时候害怕伤害他人的感情。然而持续生气的话,另一方最终也会感到受伤害,并导致关系破裂。隐藏的怨愤情绪太多会直接或间接的导致一些过激的行为和不满。你身边的人,无论是男女朋友还是夫妻,都会知道你何时生气。你有很多方式可以间接的表现出来。但是如果你不直接向他们表示你的愤怒时,他们往往会对此有所抱怨,最终失望会使人们相互疏远。

问:很多人并没意识到他们在生气,或者他们没有试图表达出来。人们怎样才能意识到自己是否表达清楚了自己的愤怒呢?

答:让人们识别自己是否在生气的一个方法就是他们是否是急脾气,如果你发现自己在道路行车时按喇叭,或者不能像自己想要的那样集中精力工作,这些都能表示已经出了问题。受到刺激的感觉是潜在愤怒的明显迹象。伴随潜在愤怒的还有一些身体上的症状,例如,偏头疼、消化性溃疡、恶心、剧烈头痛。通常你的身体会告诉你是否出了问题,你正在试图掩藏自己的情绪,而不是表达出来。

问:采取什么样的步骤才能够正确宣泄自己

❼ be aware of
意识到,察觉到
❽ honk
/hɒŋk/
v. 按汽车喇叭

the right time and the right place to express these feelings. You may in fact be in the company of others when you have these angry feelings, and you may want to find a nice quiet place where you can explain and express those feelings, or tell those feelings to the person you feel has caused them or at least is directly involved with you. So, it very much is a decision.

Q: How about the trust factor? Would you have to trust somebody before you express angry feelings to them, or does trust have anything to do with it?

A: Expressing anger is a lot easier if we trust someone. On the other hand, level of trust is not imperative[9]. We may feel angry toward a clerk in a store or a salesperson and we don't know what the level of trust is. I think the most important thing is to trust yourself. Trust your feelings and let your feelings out.

Q: For the person who hasn't learned too much about expressing anger, are there preliminary[10] steps that one can start taking to learn more about their angry feelings?

A: Yes, there is and considering it a series of steps is the easiest way to look at it. The first step is to be aware if something is going on where you are finding yourself agitated, if you are snapping at friends, if you're not doing well in your work. You know something is wrong. Give yourself time, take a few moments, and locate the source. Locating the source is the second step. Is it something you have or haven't done? Is it something inside that is going on? Or is it the result of an in-

的愤怒情绪呢？

答：当你感到生气的时候，你必须决定这是不是合适的时间和场合来宣泄自己的情绪。实际上如果你生气的时候周围有其他人，你也许想找一个安静的地方来宣泄自己的情绪，或者把自己的感觉告诉那个让你愤怒或至少与此有直接关系的人。因此，这才是明智的决定。

问：那么信任的因素呢？在你向他人宣泄情绪之前你必须要信任某人吗？或者信任与此有关系吗？

答：当你信任某人时宣泄愤怒就容易得多。另一方面，信任的程度并不十分重要。我们可能对商店里的收银员生气，也可能对推销员生气，但是我们不知道信任度有多少。我认为最重要的是要相信你自己。相信自己的感觉，释放自己的情绪。

问：对于那些不太懂得表达情绪的人有没有显著的办法让他们对自己的愤怒情绪有所了解呢？

答：是的，有。分几步考虑是认识此问题最简单的方法。第一步就是要了解到底发生了什么事情让你受到了刺激，是你跟朋友们吵了架，还自己的工作没做好。你知道出现问题了，要给自己一点儿时

---

❾ **imperative**
/ɪmˈperətɪv/
adj. 急切需要的，命令的

❿ **preliminary**
/prɪˈlɪmɪnərɪ/
adj. 初步的；预备的

teraction[11] with a friend, boyfriend, girlfriend, and spouse? The third step would be to choose the right time and the right place to express that anger. If it is anger that is inside you directed at yourself, then find a friend; check it out. See if they have the time to listen to you. Get it off your chest. If it is the result of an interaction with a certain other person, then find the right time and the right place and let them know that this is something important to you to express. And finally, number four would be to tell them your anger in the most simple, direct way you can think of. And always remember that you have the responsibility to express your anger. The other person may not respond the way you want them to — they may not be willing to hear it — but the important thing is that is their responsibility. You only have the responsibility to tell them and that's about it.

间，花几分钟找到根源。找到根源就是第二步。是不是做了什么事情或没做？或者内部有什么事情发生？或者和朋友发生了争执，无论是男女朋友还是夫妻？第三步就是要选择合适的时间和地点来宣泄愤怒。如果是对自己生气，那么就找个朋友倾诉。看看他们是否有时间倾听，然后把愤怒从胸中排除掉。如果是和其他人生气，那么就找适当的时间和地点让他们知道说出自己的愤怒是多么重要。最后第四点就是以你自己能够想到的最直接、最简单的方式说出自己的感受。并且一定要记住你有责任宣泄自己的愤怒情绪。也许另一方不会做出你能够接受的反应，他们很可能不愿意听到这些，但重要的是倾听是他们的责任。你只有告诉他们的责任。这就是关于控制愤怒。

⑪ **interaction**
/ˌɪntərˈækʃən/
n. 相互作用，相互影响

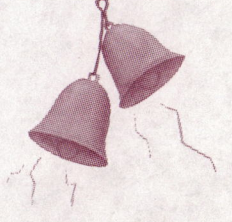

A child's cry
孩子的呐喊

Repeatedly their dreams are shattered, when again and again that parent isn't there to kiss them goodnight.

他们的梦想一次次的破碎,因为他们的父母再也没有回来亲吻过他们的额头,向他们道晚安。

Most children can't understand the meaning of Death. Their thoughts are not developed enough to process and accept its changes and finality[1]. Existence[2] continues but they long for[3] the life they once knew by hoping that soon their parent will come back to them. Repeatedly their dreams are shattered, when again and again that parent isn't there to kiss them goodnight.

As their mind works to understand the reason for them leaving, changes continue to take places causing even more confusion. Suddenly they are exposed to[4] new faces, new places and even the same is now somehow different. Soon they start to wonder how this parent, who seemed to love them so much, could leave them. The child notices the changes in the people around them as they themselves try to deal with the hurt and loss they are feeling.

By being good, they try their best to make things right again so their parent will come back home, but again they fail. The feeling of guilt mixed with the feeling of failure causes the child to feel ashamed of what they have done and they withdraw deep within themselves. They long to hide from the world in an effort to not feel, or again cause the pain that is felt so strongly by everyone around them. They become timid and shy in hopes of fading into the background so no one will find out how evil they really are.

Nights are spent lying in the dampness of silent tears that continue to fall, always haunting their thoughts of loving or being

大多数孩子不理解死亡意味着什么，因为他们的思维还没有发展到可以理解、接受事物的曲折变化和生命的终结。生活在继续，但是他们希望父母回到他们的身边，继续从前的生活。然而，他们的梦想一次次的破碎，因为他们的父母再也没有回来亲吻过他们的额头，向他们道晚安。

　　当他们的思维可以理解父母离别的原因时，周围的变化又给他们带来更多的混乱。突然，他们发现自己置身于陌生的面孔、陌生的环境，置身于那些其实相同而现在却显得那么陌生的环境里。他们想不明白为什么深爱他们父母却离开了他们。那种受伤害和失落的感觉在他们心中徘徊，他们注意到周围人在发生着变化。

　　他们努力成为好孩子，希望父母回到他们的身边，但是他们的希望又一次破碎了。强烈的内疚感和挫败感交织在一起，这些孩子开始对自己的所为感到羞愧，并且开始深深的掩藏自己的感情。他们希望与外界隔离，只有这样他们才会觉得不会给他周围的人带来伤痛。他们开始变得胆小而害羞，刻意避开公众的注意，以便没有人会发现他们内心的罪恶。

　　潮湿的泪水伴随他们度过了一个个无眠的夜晚。每晚，他们的脑海中都萦绕着一个问

❶ finality
/faɪˈnælətɪ/
n. 终结，定局
❷ existence
/ɪɡˈzɪstəns/
n. 生活，存在
❸ long for
渴望，追求
❹ be exposed to
暴露于

loved. Soon they began to feel unworthy of receiving love, but mostly they feel that they are unable to give love. They vow that they will never be hurt again and spend their life trying to avoid the love that was once felt so much. They guard their hearts, longing for a life of loneliness to save them from hurting. Unknowingly they punish themselves by blocking out the signs that love does exist in their lives. If by chances love is ever felt, caution kicks in and causes them to subconsciously drive a wedge[5] between them and the receptor of their love.

Maybe someday the child inside will find a person who is strong enough to break down the walls that have been built to protect them from the hurt. Someone, who's enduring enough to pursue the love despite the torment and the torture[6] that is thrust upon them[7] from the hurting child inside. Someone to finally release the love that's been bottled up[8] for so long, then after setting it free, basting in it's flow as it surrounds them.

The child waits inside, hiding the tears from the world and hoping each day that they will soon be set free, longing to release from their hearts years of guilt. Each night they pray for that special someone who will be strong enough, loving enough and patient enough to accept them for who they are and teach them that they are worthy of being loved. Waiting, they live their life in the darkness of the past, praying for the light of love.

题：什么是爱与被爱。很快他们觉得接受别人的爱是没有价值的，但是他们也承认自己也没有能力把爱给予别人。他们发誓不许自己再受到任何伤害，因此，他们不让自己去触摸那份曾经历的强烈的爱，他们愿与孤独为伴以保护自己不再受伤害。但是他们不知道，他们正在惩罚着自己，因为，他们拒绝、扼杀了他们生命中确实出现的爱的迹象和征兆。如果偶然间，有人表示出对他们的关爱，他们会非常小心谨慎地审视，并且故意给这些人找麻烦。

也许有一天，会有这么一位可以走进孩子内心世界的人，并且帮他们打破修筑的防范他人的"围墙"。也许，终有一天，会有一个人，锲而不舍的给予那些情感受到伤害的孩子不断的关爱，尽管他会受到来自这些孩子的许多折磨。也许，终有一天，某个孩子会把封存很久的爱全部释放出来，感情一旦释放，便倾泻出来。

孩子独自饮泣地等待着那个人的出现，他们希望很快便能解脱出来，从年复一年的内疚感中解脱出来。每个夜晚，他们祈祷着那个伟大的、有足够耐心、有足够爱心的人把他们解救出来，接受真实的他们，告诉他们自己是值得被关爱的。他们在自己黑暗的生活中等待着，祈求着爱的阳光。

❺ drive a wedge between sb.
挑拨（同事、朋友）造成不和

❻ torment and torture
折磨，痛苦

❼ sth. be thrust upon sb.
迫使某人接受某物

❽ bottle up
抑制情感

An unforgettable story
令人难忘的故事

As the enormity of his crime began to gnaw at his conscience, the trunk began to take on a human form.

强烈的罪恶性感侵蚀着他的良心,他刀下的树干这时渐渐变成了人形。

On the Swedish-speaking west coast of Finland, a church in the small town of Vora has been the heart of the farming community for centuries. My father, born in Vora in 1888, often told his children what an important role this church played for the townspeople. It was the center of religious and social life, as well as the place where births, marriages, and deaths were carefully recorded. My father's parents and siblings — three brothers and a sister — were all laid to rest beneath a black marbie tombstone in the town graveyard which lies in the shadow of the church.

I remembered that my father ever told me a remarkable story that had been passed down orally, from generation to generation, by the inhabitants of Vora —

In 1517, the German theologian[1] Martin Luther published his theses attacking the papal sales of indulgences[2] (forgiveness for sins). This sparked a religious revolution that split Europe in two, with Catholics eventually dominating the south and Reformers the north.

In the northern town of Vora, the church priest was still Catholic and had been dispensing indulgences for a price. In fact, he was becoming so prosperous that an indignant member of the congregation[3] devised a scheme to divest him of his wealth.

This wily[4] individual approached the priest and begged him to allow an indulgence for a crime he had committed! It was an unusual request, but the priest granted it.

在讲着瑞典语的芬兰西海岸，小城 Vora 有一个教堂。几个世纪以来，这个教堂都是农业种植园区的中心。我的父亲于 1888 年生于这个小镇，常常给孩子们讲述这个教堂曾经发挥的重要作用。它是当地人们宗教和社会生活的中心，也是婚丧庆典的举行之地。爸爸的父母以及他的兄弟姐妹都埋葬在这个教堂附近的小城的墓地，长眠于黑色大理石墓碑下。

记得父亲曾经给我们讲过这样一个当地人代代口口相传的故事。

1517 年，德国神学家马丁·路德提出了自己的理论来攻击教皇出售的"赎罪卷"。此举引发了宗教革命，并使得欧洲宗教一分为二，天主教最后在南方成为普遍的信仰，改革派的观点成为北方的信仰。

小镇 vora 的北部，牧师仍旧信奉天主教，而且一直在给百姓出售"赎罪卷"。事实上，他们从中获取利益，因而变得非常富有。因此，其中一位愤慨的会众，设计了巧妙方法，计划去剥夺他的财富。

这狡猾的人前去拜访牧师，并且央求牧师赦免他所犯的罪行。这是一个很离谱的请求，但是牧师答应了。付完钱后，这个被赦免的罪人，抽出藏好的刀杀掉了这位出售给他赎罪卷

❶ **theologian**
/ˌθiːəˈləʊdʒɪən/
n. 神学家
❷ **indulgence**
/ɪnˈdʌldʒəns/
n. 宽容，赦免，特赦
❸ **congregation**
/ˌkɒŋɡrɪˈɡeɪʃən/
n.（参加宗教礼拜式的）会众
❹ **wily**
/ˈwaɪlɪ/
adj. 狡猾的

As soon as he had paid the priest, the absolved[5] sinner drew out a concealed knife and murdered his pardoner. He had intended then to rob the priest of his money, but an observer who had been concealed in a dark corner of the chapel cried out, causing him to flee from the church and into the woodlands beyond. There he hid for many days, hungry and fearful, until his mother, who had been searching at night, found him. She returned with bread and cheese, and a sharp knife to slice it. Then she left him alone again.

To occupy the long hours of solitude, the man used his knife to whittle the trunk of a fallen tree. As the enormity[6] of his crime began to gnaw[7] at his conscience, the trunk began to take on a human form. During the following weeks, he was a man obsessed[8] — cutting, gouging, and paring. When his mother came back with more food, she was astonished to see what her son had carved: the body of the crucified[9] Christ!

At his mother's urging, the man returned to the church, full of contrition[10], and offered up the work of art as an act of atonement[11]. The townspeople proclaimed it a masterpiece, but whether the church would accept or display the work of such a wicked person was a matter of great debate. They finally decided to suspend the statue within the sanctuary, but at a discreet distance from the altar, about 30 feet. This is where it has hung ever since.

The local people of Vora accept the tale as irrefutable[12] truth, it should not be questioned. Besides, it does make for an incredibly good story.

的牧师。他本想把牧师的钱财一起掠走，但是有个人一直藏在小教堂的黑暗角落里，这时他大声疾呼。仓皇之下，他逃离了教堂，逃到了森林里。那里，他忍饥挨饿，在惊慌恐惧中度过了许多天。直到有一天夜里，他的母亲找到这里发现了他。他的母亲回到家中，给他带来了面包、奶酪、和一把切面包片的刀。之后，他又一个人孤零零地待在那儿了。

为了排解孤独难熬的时间，他用这把刀刻削一个倒在地上的树干。强烈的罪恶感侵蚀着他的良心，这时，他刀下的树干渐渐变成了人形。接下来的几周，他简直沉迷于自己的工作——切割、凿洞、修边。当他的母亲带着食物来看他时，她惊讶地发现她的儿子雕刻了一个钉在十字架上的耶稣。

在母亲的劝说下，他满怀忏悔地回到了教堂，并把他雕刻的这份作品作为赎罪品上交了。镇里的人承认这是个杰作，但是，他们激烈地讨论着能否接受或者是展览这个罪恶深重的人雕刻的作品。最后，他们决定把这个雕塑立在圣堂里，但与祭坛保持一段的距离，约30英尺。从此它就一直摆放在那里。

当地的许多人，对这个传说没有一点儿怀疑。不管怎么说，这是一个奇妙的故事。

❺ absolve
/əbˈzɒlv/
v. 宣布免除，解除

❻ enormity
/ɪˈnɔːmɪtɪ/
n. 严重罪行

❼ gnaw
/nɔː/
v. 折磨

❽ obsess
/əbˈses/
v. 着迷，牵挂

❾ crucify
/ˈkruːsɪfaɪ/
v. 把…钉死在十字架上

❿ contrition
/kənˈtrɪʃən/
n. 忏悔

⓫ atonement
/əˈtəʊnmənt/
n. 赎罪

⓬ irrefutable
/ɪˈrefjʊtəbl/
adj. 驳不倒的

The story of Julia
朱莉娅的故事

Everyone looked up to him for his great wisdom and healing powers.

村子里有一个智慧非凡且具有某种治愈力量的智人，大家都非常景仰他。

Once upon a time...

There was a woman named Julia who lived in a small village in a small kingdom. She worked very hard. She had inside of her a sort of yearning to be a pertness[1] of life, but she always had much work to do. She thought that was what she should do: take care of others, and be a good responsible person.

Then one day an evil wizard[2] came to her cottage and put a curse on her so that she worked harder and harder and never got any rest, time to enjoy life, or even take care of herself, until she was very tired and very sick. She went to see a wise man in the village to see if he could help her; everyone looked up to him for his great wisdom and healing powers. He told her he could give her magic potion[3] to take the curse away.

Julia became even sicker when she took the magic potion. She could no longer work and had to rest and take care of herself. But soon she began to feel better, and something mysterious and exciting was happening to Julia! As the curse left her body, her yearning for life also emerged. Her life took on a radiance[4] she had never known before!

The sky appeared as splendid as heaven to her. The birds sang like a symphony orchestra. Her home resembled a castle. A simple picnic tasted like a banquet dinner. Fields of wildflowers smelled like the palace raised gardens. All the things she touched felt soft fine furs. Her family became as resplendent[5] as royalty.

朱莉娅的故事

很久很久以前……

一个叫朱莉娅的妇女住在一个小国的小村庄里,她每天都勤勤恳恳的工作。在她内心深处,她渴望过上精致、悠闲的生活,但是她每天都有许许多多工作要做:照顾别人,力求做一个有责任感的人,所有的这些她都觉得是应该做的。

一天一个邪恶的巫师来到她的小农舍给她施了魔咒,从此她比平时更加马不停蹄的工作;没有时间休息,没有时间享受生活,甚至腾不出时间照顾自己,最后她筋疲力尽,终于累倒了。村子里有一个智慧非凡且具有某种治愈力量的智人,大家都非常景仰他。最后朱丽叶向这位智人寻求帮助,他给了朱莉娅一些有魔力的药剂,并告诉她这些药可以驱除魔咒。

喝下这些药后,她病得更重了,她再也不能下地干活必须躺在床上休息,调养自己。但是很快,她就觉得好多了,她感受到了一些神奇的,令人激动的东西。魔咒解除后,生活的热情在心中重新点燃,她的生活从来没有这样灿烂过。

对她来说,天空就像天堂一样华丽,鸟儿的歌就像交响乐团弹奏出来一样的动听,她的小屋就像城堡一样漂亮,简单的野餐就像宴席一样可口,路边的野花闻起来就如宫

❶ **pertness**
/ˈpɜːtnɪs/
n. 雅致,时髦

❷ **wizard**
/ˈwɪzəd/
n. 男巫

❸ **potion**
/ˈpəʊʃn/
n. 一服药水

❹ **radiance**
/ˈreɪdɪəns/
n. 灿烂,发光

❺ **resplendent**
/rɪˈsplendənt/
adj. 华丽灿烂的

Her husband appeared as handsome and charming as the prince of the kingdom. And her friends were transformed into[6] elegant kings and queens. She laughed more often, sang beautiful songs, danced lovely dances. She loved the new life magic potion and the wise man seemed to have brought to her. She knew from then on that she needed to take care of herself, love herself, and love life.

"And what about the future?" she asked the wise man. "Will the curse return? Will I need more of your magic? Will I live like this forever? Will I die?"

And the wise man answered, "Although I have studied long and hard and know many things, I do not know the answers to your questions. The curse may still be lurking[7] quietly inside of you waiting to take over your life again, and it may do so, and you may die. But in the meantime, if you believe in the power of the magic, you will love life and find treasures in those around you worth more than all the gold in the kingdom! You now have the power to make the magic yourself. It is your choice, Julia. You may accept your magic for today with no promises or guarantees for the future, or you can spend today in fear that the curse will return. It Is your choice, Julia."

Julia listened intently[8]. She knew that her life would never be the same as it had been before the curse had been put on her. She felt a part of life and all the riches it had to offer.

殿里的花香，触摸到所有东西，她都觉得温软。她的家像皇宫一样华丽灿烂，她的丈夫就像王子一样英俊迷人，她周围的朋友有如高雅的国王和王后，她变得爱笑、爱唱、爱跳了。她热爱这个魔力的药剂、她热爱智人带给她的这种快乐生活，从那以后，她知道她应该照料自己、爱护自己，而且热爱生活。

"未来会怎样呢？"她问这个智者，"魔咒还会重新降临吗？我是否需要更多的魔力呢？我能否永远这样快乐的生活下去？我会死吗？"

那位智者回答道："尽管我认真研究很久，而且知道许多事情，但是我还是不知道如何回答你的问题。魔咒还有可能潜藏在你心中，而且可能再次控制你的生活，如果这样，你有可能就会死去。但是，如果你相信我给你的魔力，你就会热爱生活而且会发现你周围的东西比国王宫中的黄金更有价值；现在你自己有这种力量去制造这种魔力，那是你自己的选择，朱莉娅：不对明天做出承诺和保证，就在今天接爱魔力，去享受现在的快乐；或者是惧怕魔咒再次来临的状态中度过今天。朱莉娅这是你自己的选择。"

朱莉娅认真地听着，她知道，与魔咒控制她生活之前相比，她今后的生活将大大不同。现在她感受到了生活的丰富多彩。

❻ transform into
v. 变为
❼ lurk
/lɜːk/
v. 潜伏
❽ intently
/ɪnˈtentlɪ/
adv. 专注地

The potter
制陶工人

The ceramic pots were still piled up high, and that same smile shone brightly under the afternoon sun. Nothing had changed.

瓷器还是和从前一样堆得高高的,那一模一样的微笑在午后的阳光下绽放得还是那么光彩照人。什么都没有改变。

情感篇

We often set sail into the great big world with high expectations. If you're lucky, you return with a smile on your face. If not, well ...

I wish I knew then what I know now. Then, perhaps, I wouldn't have wasted all those years.

It was almost a decade ago, and I had just finished college. With my degree in hand, and a truckload of ego[1] and confidence, I donned slick[2] designer clothes to impress during my first interview.

The building where I had to go for the interview was one I hadn't heard of before. Feeling miffed[3] that the weather in my country shines kindly only upon cotton and loose clothing, I wished I could have stayed on in Australia. Then I wouldn't have to think twice about wearing thick (and expensive!) suits.

As I furiously[4] wiped the sweat off my sticky face, I came to an old building.

I looked around for an air-conditioned partition, an office maybe. However, all I saw was a huge collection of ceramic pots, and a man sitting amidst the clutter. The slight, sun burnt person smiled and squinted his eyes. He stopped work to look at me.

As I approached him and showed him the paper with the address of the building I wanted, he didn't budge at all. But he blinked[5] once or twice because of the glaring sun. And that smile

我们经常怀有很大的希望到我们的这个世俗世界去冲浪、淘金，你可能很幸运，会面带微笑衣锦还乡，如果运气不好的话，……

要是之前就能够明白现在的那些事，也许，我就不会荒废这么多年了。

十年前，我大学刚毕业，手持我的大学文凭，穿着一身笔挺、光滑的设计师服装，浑身洋溢着自我和自信，去迎接我的第一个面试。

这之前，我没有听说过这个我将要面试的地方。一想到家乡的天气能够把棉制或宽大的衣服，照得流光溢彩我就禁不住有点儿恼火。这时真的希望自己是在澳大利亚，因为在那儿我就不用去为了穿一身厚点儿（而且很贵）的西服而前思后想了。

我恼火地揩去脸上的汗水，这时我来到了一幢旧楼前。

我四下找寻着带有空调的隔间，也可以说是在找办公室。然而，我看到的却是一排排瓷器。一个人就坐在这些乱七八糟的东西之间，他的皮肤被轻微晒伤，他停下了手里的活儿，面带微笑、眯着眼看着我。

我朝他走去，拿出一张纸给他看，纸上写着我想要到的那个地址。但是，他没有丝毫反应，刺眼的光线使他眨了眨眼睛，脸上

❶ **ego**
/ˈiːɡəʊ/
n. 自我

❷ **slick**
/slɪk/
adj. 平滑的，光滑的

❸ **miffed**
/mɪfd/
adj. 恼怒的，生气的

❹ **furiously**
/ˈfjʊərɪəslɪ/
adv. 狂暴地

❺ **blink**
/blɪŋk/
v. 眨眼

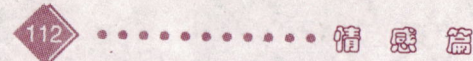

stayed on his face.

"Do you know where this is?" I asked rather importantly, like I was late for a crucial meeting.

He looked at the paper, then at me, and his smile grew wider.

"Where is it? Do you know or not?" I was getting impatient.

"It is here," he replied.

I was almost speechless. All my time wasted, and my best clothes ... only to encounter[6] this small person.

"Where's your boss?" I asked, hoping that he'd show me to a shiny flashy block behind the stack of ceramics.

"Everybody here helps make and sell our pots. We are looking for someone to meet and speak to our distributors[7]. You want the job?" asked the man, who turned out to be the owner of the ceramics center.

With one eyebrow raised, I turned and didn't look back. I was angry with him for not being specific in the classified ads. I was angry, too, that the weather was so hot.

Later that week, I found my stylish job at a multinational firm and was happy. But after a few weeks, I felt that the new friends I

还是挂着那种微笑。

"你知道这是哪儿吗?"我郑重其事地向他询问着,就好像要耽误了一个非常重要的会议一样。

他看看纸,又看看我,笑得更厉害了。

"到底是哪儿?知不知道呀?"我变得很不耐烦。

"就是这儿。"他答道。

啊?当时简直气得说不出话来,我的时间、我最好的衣服都白废了。最后却只是见到了这么一个身材矮小的人。

"老板在哪儿?"我问道。希望在这一堆堆瓷器后面,能看到一个亮闪、华丽的隔间。

"这儿的每个人都制作、销售这些罐罐。我们正在找一个能和我们的批发商接洽的人,你想做这事?"他问道。俨然,他是这里的老板。

我眉毛一翘,头也不回地转身便走。我非常气愤,因为他的广告太不细致、太不具体了,我也非常恼火,因为这儿的天气太闷热。

之后,我在一家跨国公司找到一份有格调的工作,我兴奋无比。但是几周后,我却发现,我在那里新交的朋友,除了他们自己和他们的工作,什么也不关心。几个月后,

6 encounter
/ɪnˈkaʊntə/
v. 遇到
7 distributor
/dɪˈstrɪbjʊtə/
n. 分销商

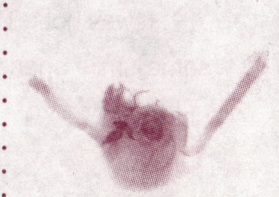

made there didn't really care for much except themselves and their work. After a few months, I realized, too, that I didn't care for much except my high-paying job and myself.

And no matter how much more I earned, there was always some-thing new to buy. Something to keep me happy, for a few days at least?

The months soon turned into years, years filled with jealousy, hatred[8], and that unquenchable[9] hunger for more. There were times when I wanted to call it quits because I wasn't sure if this road I had taken was worth it.

Then, last month, I was assigned to return to my hometown to meet a new client. The address looked familiar.

On my way there, my suspicions were confirmed: I would be dealing with the ceramics boss. I quickly figured a way to handle things smoothly. I would pretend that I've never met him before.

I felt at ease again as I walked in and saw him, crouched over some pots, his hands caked with clay[10].

It was hot. The ceramic pots were still piled up high, and that same smile shone brightly under the afternoon sun. Nothing had changed.

我也意识到，除了我自己和我的高薪工作，我也什么都不关心。

不论我比以前多挣了多少，我总是有新的东西要买。一些事能让我开心幸福吗，哪怕几天也好？

月月相继，年复一年，岁月里充斥着嫉妒、愤恨和无法满足的利欲。好几次，我都想退出，因为我不能够确定，这条路我是否选择正确。

之后，上个月，公司指派我回家乡会见一个新的顾客商，地址看起来这么眼熟。

路上，我的怀疑得到了证实，我将要和那个瓷器老板打交道。很快我便想出了一个两全齐美的方法，那就是，假装以前没有见过他。

当我再次走进这间楼房时，我感到很轻松。我看到他正蹲在瓷罐中间，手上沾满了黏土。

天气很热。瓷器还是和从前一样堆得高高的，那一模一样的微笑在午后的阳光下绽放得还是那么光彩照人。什么都没有改变。

我介绍了一下我自己，在商讨文件前，我佯装笑了笑。当我打开公文包时，我注意到这个身材矮小的人在盯着我看，我抬头看见他像个傻瓜一样笑着。

❽ **hatred**
/ˈheɪtrɪd/
n. 仇恨

❾ **unquenchable**
/ˌʌnˈkwentʃəbl/
adj. 无法扑来的

❿ **clay**
/kleɪ/
n. 黏土

I introduced myself, and flashed my fake smile before proceeding to the documents. As I opened my briefcase, I noticed the small man looking at me. I looked up and saw him smiling like a fool.

I forgot that he was a client and blurted, "What? Why are you always smiling?"

I felt a horrible sense of regret. Yet, there was relief for it had been a long time since I last lashed out in frustration.

He said to me, "I've almost finished with this piece. See. This bowl was first gathered from the ground, wet, and then kneaded to perfection. After that, I burnt it in the kiln[11], watching it closely to ensure the temperature was not too hot. Then I left it to cool. When it is ready, I will stroke its comforting crimson[12] body."

When he finished talking, the man held up the ceramic pot. I took it from him for a closer look. Yes, even though it wasn't quite finished, the pot looked beautiful.

"Be careful. If it drops, all that's left will be the broken pieces. If you glue it back, it will never be the same again. But you can still change its appearance. All you need is some paint, and some more time. Do you mind waiting for me while I finish?" the man asked.

I looked at him, smiled, and nodded my head.

我忘了他是我们的顾客，脱口便说："你为什么总笑？"

说完这话，我感到很后悔。然而，那种积压很久的沮丧，这时得到了极大的放松和排解。

他对我说："我快完成这件瓷器了。看，首先用湿泥巴先弄出一个碗的形状，然后再捏成比较完美的形状，之后，我在窑里烧烘它，这时要紧紧地盯着它，以确保烧烘的温度不要太高，然后拿出来冷却一会儿，然后就要釉上迷人的深红色。"

他介绍完后，拿起他的瓷器，我拿过来仔细看，尽管还没完全做完，但是这个瓷器已经很漂亮了。

"拿住了，别摔了，一旦摔下去，就碎成了一片片。重新粘它，也不可能回复到之前的样子，但是你可以给它改头换面，而你所需要的就是时间和漆刷。你介意等我把活儿做完吗？"他问我。

我微笑地看着他，点了点头。

⑪ kiln
/kɪln/
n. 烧窑

⑫ crimson
/ˈkrɪmzən/
adj. 深红色的

You sure are lucky
你一定会有好运

With much reverence and ceremony, he slowly removed my hat with both hands and presented it to me as though it were the crown jewels.

他用两只小手慢慢地把帽子取下，有如手捧王冠一样，他以一种非常崇敬的礼节方式把帽子还给了我。

It was a hot, muggy[1] August afternoon, and I had every reason to feel sorry for myself. A comedy of hassles[2] began with the normal airport security gauntlet, followed by a random drug test, and a missed flight home due to a number of mechanical, weather problems.

During the usual pandemonium[3] at the gate, I noticed a 5-year-old boy standing by his mother and watching me. He looked at me, then my bag, then back at me.

Cautiously, he left his mother's side and slowly began to walk toward me, glancing between my bag, his mother, and me. As he came closer, I was both relieved and alarmed that it wasn't me he was after. It was my hat.

I started to tell him not to bother my things, but something made me stop and watch. He stopped in front of my bag, looking at my hat, then up at me.

With wide eyes, he gently touched the bill[4] of my hat. Running his index finger slowly along the edge, carefully touching the emblem[5].

Again, he looked up at me, now smiling, but saying nothing. I asked him if he would like to wear my captain hat. He excitedly nodded his head, still smiling. I placed my hat on his head, but it fell down around his ears. He didn't seem to mind and held it up in the proper position with both hands. He ran to show his moth-

在一个闷热而潮湿的秋季下午，我有足够的理由同情我自己。争吵混乱的闹剧从飞机的安检开始，紧接着是抽样药检，然后是由于天气因素和机械故障造成的误点航班。

登机口一片混乱与喧闹，这时我注意到一个 5 岁的小男孩，他站在妈妈的身边盯着我。他看看我，看看我的提包，再看看我。

他小心谨慎地离开妈妈那边，慢慢地向我走来，他不时地看着我，看看他妈妈和我的提包。他靠近我时，我才发现他并不是冲着我而是冲着我的帽子来的。这既让我宽慰许多，又让我感到奇怪。

我本想告诉他不要乱动我的东西，但是我也不知道为什么我没去拦他，而是想看看他究竟要做什么。他在我的提包前停下，看看我的帽子，然后抬头看看我。

他的眼睛很大。他轻轻地摸了摸我的帽沿，食指慢慢地沿着帽沿划来划去，然后小心地摸着帽子的徽章。

他抬起头来笑咪咪的看着我，但是没有说话，我问他想不想戴戴我的上尉帽子，他激动地连连点头，脸上还挂着那种微笑。我把帽子扣在他头上，帽子一下滑到他的耳际，但是他丝毫不介意，两只小手把帽子调到合适的位置。他跑过去给他的妈妈看，然后又

❶ **muggy**
/ˈmʌgɪ/
adj. 闷热而潮湿的

❷ **hassle**
/ˈhæsl/
n. 困难，争吵

❸ **pandemonium**
/ˌpændɪˈməunjəm/
n. 大混乱，喧闹

❹ **bill**
/bɪl/
n. 帽沿

❺ **emblem**
/ˈembləm/
n. 徽章

er, then back to me still <u>smiling from ear to ear</u>[6].

With much reverence[7] and ceremony, he slowly removed my hat with both hands and presented it to me as though it were the crown jewels.

I put my hat on and gave him an airplane card. This, too, he held with both hands in awe.

After this exchange, he still hadn't spoken, although I knew he was excited. I also was happy that I had been briefly distracted[8] from my self-pity fester[9].

Still holding the card carefully with both hands, he looked up at me and said, "Mister, you sure are lucky."

"Yes," I said, "I sure am."

I contemplated[10] the wisdom of a 5-year-old, as I got the last seat on that flight home.

眉开眼笑地跑回来。

他用两只小手慢慢地把帽子取下,有如手捧王冠一样,他以一种非常崇敬的礼节方式把帽子还给了我。

我戴上帽子,给了他一张明信片,他仍旧是充满崇敬地用双手捧住。

拿到这张明信片后,他非常激动,但是他还是没有说话。其实,我也非常高兴,因为他把我从坏心境中拉拽了出来。

两只小手仍然小心捧着明信片,他抬起头来看看我对我说:"先生,你一定会有好运的。"

"是的,"我说:"我肯定。"

我是最后一个坐到座位上的人,在返乡的飞行中,我思考着那5岁小男孩话中的智慧。

❻ smile from ear to ear
眉开眼笑
❼ reverence
/ˈrevərəns/
n. 尊敬,敬畏
❽ distract
/dɪsˈtrækt/
v. 分散,分神
❾ fester
/ˈfestə/
n.(怨恨等)郁积
❿ comtemplate
/ˈkɒntempleɪt/
v. 沉思

Return to Paradise
重返伊甸园

She began to believe that maybe she had a future after all and maybe it could be with this man, with his kind hazel eyes, wet with their shared tears.

她想到她会有自己的明天，也许可以和这个长着褐色眼睛的男人一起分担忧愁。

Lisa gazed out over the Caribbean Sea, feeling the faint breeze against her face — eyes shut, the white sand warm between her bare toes. The place was beautiful beyond belief, but it was still unable to ease the grief[1] she felt as she remembered the last time she had been here.

She had married James right here on this spot three years ago to the day. Dressed in a simple white shift dress, miniature white roses attempting to tame her long dark curls, Lisa had been happier than she had ever thought possible. James was even less formal but utterly irresistible[2] in creased summer trousers and a loose white cotton shirt. His dark hair slightly ruffled and his eyes full of adoration as his looked at his bride[3] to be. The <u>justice of the peace</u>[4] had read their vows as they held hands and laughed at the sheer joy of being young, in love and staying in a five star resort on the Caribbean island of the Dominican Republic. They had seen the years blissfully stretching ahead of them, together forever. They planned their children, two she said, he said four, so they compromised on three (two girls and a boy of course); where they would live, the travelling they would do together — it was all certain, so they had thought then.

But that seemed such a long time ago now. A lot can change in just a few years — a lot of heartache can change a person and drive a wedge through the strongest ties, break even the deepest love. Three years to the day and they had returned, though this time not for the beachside marriages the island was famous for but for one of its equally popular quickie divorces.

莉萨凝望着加勒比海，闭上双眼感受迎面吹来的微风，温暖的细沙缠绕在她的脚趾间。这个地方美得无与伦比，但是想起上次的情景，她心中的悲伤就难以抚平。

就在三年前，就在这里，她与詹姆斯举行了婚礼。一袭白色的连衣裙，一支小小的白色玫瑰别在她又长又黑的卷发上，那一刻她无比幸福。詹姆斯的着装也很随意，比挺的夏日长裤配上一件宽松的纯棉白色衬衫。他的黑色头发有点儿乱。他充满深情地注视着他的新娘。一名治安法官是他们的证婚人。他们手拉手，宣告着誓言，沉浸在爱情和青春以及住在多米尼加的五星级度假胜地的无比幸福的感觉里，幸福的笑声洒满整个沙滩。他们展望着他们的幸福时光，他们计划着要几个孩子的问题，她说两个，他说四个，最后他们决定要三个（两个女孩，一个男孩）。他们计划着今后住在哪里以及去哪里旅游度假的问题，这是一定的事，所以他们那时就开始盘算了。

但是那一切似乎距现在已经那么久远了。几年内，物是人非，一件件让人心痛的事可以改变一个人，可以击碎最亲密的关系，甚至可以破坏最深最深的爱情。三年后，他们重返这片以举行沙滩婚礼而驰名的海滩，这

❶ **grief**
/griːf/
n. 悲伤，忧伤

❷ **irresistible**
/ˌɪrɪˈzɪstəbl/
adj. 难以抵抗的

❸ **bride**
/braɪd/
n. 新娘

❹ **justice of the peace**
n. 治安法官

Lisa let out a sigh that was filled with pain and regret. What could she do but move on, find a new life and new dreams? — the old one was beyond repair. How could this beautiful place, with its lush[5] green coastline, eternity of azure[6] blue sea and endless sands be a place for the agony she felt now?

The man stood watching from the edge of the palm trees. He couldn't take his eyes of the dark-haired woman he saw standing at the water's edge, gazing out to sea as though she was waiting for something — or someone. She was beautiful, with her slim figure dressed in a loose flowing cotton dress, her crazy hair and bright blue eyes not far off the color of the sea itself. It wasn't her looks that attracted him though; he came across many beautiful women in his work as a freelance photographer. It was her loneliness and intensity that lured him. Even at some distance he was aware that she was different from any other woman he could meet.

Lisa sensed the man approaching even before she turned around. She had been aware of him standing there staring at her and had felt strangely calm about being observed. She looked at him and felt the instant spark[7] of connection she had only experienced once before. He walked slowly towards her and they held each other's gaze. It felt like meeting a long lost friend — not a stranger on a strange beach.

Later, sitting at one of the many bars on the resort, sipping the local cocktails they began to talk. First pleasantries[8], their ho-

一次，他们却来这里结束她们的婚姻。

　　莉萨悲伤地叹了口气，她现在能做的只能是继续前进寻找新的生活、新的梦想吗？然而旧的伤痕还没愈合。为什么这片繁茂的绿色海岸线，亘古永恒的蔚蓝色的海洋，和无边无垠的沙滩现在却让她如此心痛？

　　一位男士站在棕榈树下远远望着她，他的视线无法从她身上离开，这位有着一头黑发凝望着大海的女人，仿佛正在等候着什么事情或者说什么人。她非常漂亮，苗条的身材被一袭棉制长裙包裹着，她蓬乱的头发和那双明亮的眼睛几乎与大海颜色融为一体。尽管这样，并不是她的美丽吸引了他，他是个摄影师，由于工作关系，他能接触到许多漂亮女人。吸引他的是她那强烈地孤独感，即使距离很远他也能感受她和他之前遇到的女人不同。

　　没有转身莉萨已经感觉到有人在向他走来。她早已察觉到他站在那儿一直看着她，但是这一次被别人观察时，她却出奇地冷静。抬头看了看他，瞬间，曾经有过的那种亲密的感觉突然迸发出来。他慢慢向她走去，彼此凝望着对方，那种感觉仿佛是遇到了许久没有联系的朋友，而不是在陌生的沙滩上见到一个陌生人。

　　之后，他们选了一家酒吧，品着鸡尾酒，

❺ lush
/lʌf/
adj. 繁茂的

❻ azure
/'æʒə/
adj. 蔚蓝色

❼ spark
/spɑːk/
n. 火花

❽ pleasantry
/'plezəntrɪ/
轻松幽默的话

tels, the quality of the food and friendliness of the locals. Their conversation was strangely hesitant considering the naturalness[9] and confidence of their earlier meeting. Onlookers, however, would have detected the subtle flirtation[10] as they mirrored each other's actions and spoke directly into each other's eyes. Only later, after the alcohol had had its loosening effect, did the conversation deepen. They talked of why they were here and finally, against her judgment, Lisa opened up about her heartache of the past year and how events had led her back to the place where she had married the only man she believed she could ever love. She told him of things that had been locked deep inside her, able to tell no one. She told him how she had felt after she had lost her baby.

She was six months pregnant and the happiest she had ever been when the pains had started. She was staying with her mother as James was working out of town. He hadn't made it back in time. The doctor had said it was just one of those things, that they could try again. But how could she when she couldn't even look James in the eye. She hated him then, for not being there, for not hurting as much as her but most of all for looking so much like the tiny baby boy that she held for just three hours before he took him away. All through the following months she had withdrawn from her husband, family, friends. Not wanting to recover from the pain she felt — that would have been a betrayal of her son. At the funeral she had refused to stand next to her husband and the next day she had left him.

Looking up, Lisa could see her pain reflected in the man's

他们开始聊了起来。开始时他们谈轻松幽默的话题，评价他们下榻的旅店、这里的食物以及当地人的友好。偶然的邂逅以及对彼此的不太信任，使得谈话一开始有点儿拘谨。但是，当他们目视着对方交谈时，当他们注视着彼此的行为时，旁观者分明会发现他们在调情。后来酒精起到了作用，他们的谈话深入了许多。他们讲述着来这里的目的，明知这样不好，莉萨还是向他倾诉了自己过去一年里的伤心往事，以及什么事情使她回到这片她和丈夫曾经举行婚礼的地方。在这儿，她嫁给了她认为会相爱一生一世的男人。她诉说了封存在心底的许多事情，而这些从没向别人提起过，她对他讲述当她失去孩子时的那种感觉。

她怀孕六个月，便早产了，分娩那一刻是她最幸福的一刻。当时詹姆斯不在城里工作，她只好与母亲住在一起，那天他没有及时赶回来。医生说没事，他们还可以再要个孩子，但是再也不想看到詹姆斯了，又如何提起再要个孩子。她恨他，恨他当时不在，恨他就像恨自己只能让小男婴存活三个小时。接下来的几个月，她刻意回避她的丈夫、家庭和朋友。她不想让自己从悲伤中恢复过来，因为她觉得那是对儿子的背叛。丧礼上，他拒绝与丈

⑨ naturalness
/ˈnætʃərəlnɪs/
n. 自然性

⑩ flirtation
/flɜːˈteɪʃən/
n. 调情

eyes. For the first time in months she didn't feel alone, she felt the unbearable[11] burden begin to lift from her, only a bit but it was a start. She began to believe that maybe she had a future after all and maybe it could be with this man, with his kind hazel[12] eyes, wet with their shared tears.

They had come here to dissolve[13] their marriage but maybe there was hope. Lisa stood up and took James by the hand and led him away from the bar towards the beach where they had made their vows to each other three years ago. Tomorrow she would cancel the divorce; tonight they would work on renewing their promises.

夫站在一起，第二天，她便离开了他。

　　她抬起头，看到了他眼中的伤痛，几个月以来第一次，她不再觉得那么孤单，她感到那不堪重负的压力正在褪去。尽管只是那么一点点，但却已经开始变化。她想到她会有自己的明天，也许可以和这个长着褐色眼睛的男人一起分担忧愁。

　　他们来到这里解除了婚姻，但是也许还有希望。莉萨站起身来抓住了詹姆斯的手走出酒吧，来到那个三年前他们海誓山盟的沙滩。明天，她要撤消离婚，今晚他们要重构彼此的诺言。

⑪ **unbearable**
/ʌnˈbeərəbl/
adj. 不堪忍受的

⑫ **hazel**
/ˈheɪzəl/
adj. 浅褐色的

⑬ **dissolve**
/dɪˈzɒlv/
v. 解除

Destiny
前生注定

All I can say is that it's destiny. How else can we explain the feeling we had from first time we met?"

我想告诉你,这就是前生注定。我们又如何解释我们初次相遇的那种感觉呢?

情感篇

I went to a convention, with a group of friends. One of the people there was my best friend Cher she brought Juan with her. We was all staying in the dorm and Cher introduced me to Juan. I was 21 at the time and I was rooming with my mother. Juan was very attractive[1], and I felt as if I knew him when I first met him. It was so strange that feeling I had and later on discovered he also had that feeling.

We became fast friends and we discovered we lived in the same town and stranger than that we lived in same apartment complex[2]. The convention was over and we all went back home. Before I dropped my mother off she said, "Kate you know that Juan is a bit older than you so be careful." I love my mother very much, but I told her, "Mom since I'm 21 which is of legal age, it really doesn't matter how old Juan is. Especially since we are just friends." My mother looked at me in that way that all mothers have a way of doing.

Of course Juan was waiting there for me, since I told him I had just bought a new computer and was having trouble putting all the doodads[3] in their proper place. We had a very nice evening. I fixed dinner and we was talking getting to know each other. I asked if he wanted to go to the store with me to develop some old film that I had bought at an auction. He just smiled and said "no need to make a trip to the store since I can develop film at my apartment." I laughed, and said "a man of many talents huh?" I told him "Really I can take it to the store since you was so kind as to help/put my computer together". That is when he

一天和一群朋友去参加一个聚会，其中我的一位好朋友切尔把胡安带来了。我们在寝室闲聊时，切尔把我介绍给胡安认识，那时我21岁，还和母亲住在一起。胡安英俊迷人，初次见面就有似曾相识之感，后来才知道，他见我的一刹那也有这种感觉。

我们很快就攀谈起来，此时，才发现我们住在同一个小镇，更让我惊讶的是，我们住在同一个社区里。聚会结束了，我们都回家了。下车前，母亲对我说："凯特，胡安可比你大，你要小心留意些。"我非常爱我的母亲，但我却说："妈妈，我已经21岁了，早已成人了，我并不在乎胡安的年龄，更何况我们只是朋友。"母亲以一种天底下所有母亲都会有的反应看着我。

当然，胡安正在等着我，因为我和他说我买了一台新电脑，但我总组装不好。我亲自准备了晚餐，我们聊着，慢慢地了解着对方，那一晚我们过得非常愉快。我问他能否顺便陪我到照相馆，冲洗我在拍卖会上买的一些老胶卷。他微笑地对我说："不用去照相馆，在我家就能帮你洗照片。"我笑道："这么多才多艺呀？"我对他说："当然，我可以自己把胶卷带到照相馆，已经很感谢你帮我把电脑组装好了。"他赶忙说道："凯特，我知道我们才刚

❶ **attractive**
/əˈtræktɪv/
adj. 有吸引力的

❷ **complex**
/ˈkɒmpleks/
n. 建筑群

❸ **doodad**
/ˈduːdæd/
n. 小装置

said "Kate I know we just met, but I feel like I've known you all of my life. Do you believe in destiny? " I just stared at him for quite a few minutes. Of all the lame pickup lines I heard this one really touched my soul. Finally I said, "Juan from the first day we met at the convention, I had this nagging[4] feeling that I also had known you all of my life." "I was afraid to sound like a big stupid, and I didn't want to scare you away before we had a chance to get to know each other." "Really Kate I don't think you could run me off with just that." He said with a twinkle in his eyes we both started laughing. "Now about this film," I said, "I'm not sure what you will find on it, if anything. I just bought it <u>on a whim</u>[5] and the price was right." I said smiling. He said, "Well if you want you can come to the apartment with me and watch me develop it and make sure that I'm very careful with it." With a twinkle in his eyes. "I promise that I will be a gentleman and not do anything that you don't want me too," He said jokingly. So we went back to his apartment and I put on some coffee for us. We went into his darkroom. I was very interested in the darkroom since I had never seen one before. I was walking around being very careful not to touch anything and admiring his photos that he took and developed, he was really an extraordinary photographer which he pointed out that it was just one of his hobbies. Like I said a man of many talents. "Kate come over here and I will show how the negatives[6] become the pictures."

"Does that mean there is something on them? " I asked with excitement. He started to work his magic with the pictures and when they started developing we both look at each other with as-

刚认识，但是我总感觉我们早已相识，你相信命运吗？"我盯着他好几分钟，这句话触动了我的内心深处，最后我说："胡安，我们第一次在聚会上见面，我就有这种不断困扰我的感觉，我觉得我们仿佛已经认识了一辈子。""我怕你笑话我傻，怕吓跑你，这样地话，我们就没有机会了解对方了。""凯特，你不会把我吓走的。"他目光熠熠地对我说。我们都笑了。"至于这个胶卷，"我说道，"不知这些胶卷照的是什么，我只是心血来潮才买了它们，而且价格也不贵。"他微笑地说："如果你能来我家，就可以看到我是怎样冲洗这些胶卷的，我会很小心的。"他眼里充满着期望看着我。"我保证我一定会像个绅士一样，不会做你不想做的事。"他开玩笑地说。我们一起来到他家，我冲了些咖啡。我对他的暗室充满了兴趣，因为之前从未见识过。我非常小心地在他的暗室走动，不敢碰任何东西，我惊叹那些他自拍自洗的照片，他简直就是一名非常优秀的摄影师，他却说摄影只是他的一项业余爱好。像我说的那样他简直就是个天才。"凯特，快过来看，看看我是怎么把底片冲成照片的。"

"胶卷里真的有东西？"我激动地问。他开始洗起了照片。照片冲好后，我们都惊诧不已的看着对方，我们盯着眼前把我们俩照

❹ **nagging**
/ˈnæɡɪŋ/
adj. 令人烦恼不已的

❺ **on a whim**
一时兴起，心血来潮

❻ **negative**
/ˈneɡətɪv/
n. 底片

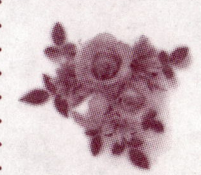

tonishment right in front of our eyes we was staring at a pictures of us, but we was dressed strangely. My hair was piled up on my head and had quite a serene[7] look on my face. I was dressed in a white lace dress that the collar went up to my neck, and in the middle of that was a cameo, he was standing beside me with his hands on my shoulders, quite dashing[8] in his coat and tie, and we both was looking so much in love. Than the next picture was us in the same outfit but him sitting and me sitting besides him <u>at an angle</u>[9] with his hands around my waist. I was speechless how could this be, I was wondering, since I know I had only met him like a week ago. Picture after picture was just the same as the first. Us there in different settings but us dressed the same as first I described. Finally I could not take it anymore. I looked up in his eyes and asked what was on my mind, "How can this be Juan? We only met each other a week ago and those pictures is of us, but in another time another life." He just smiled at and looked at me the same way that dashing man was looking at the lady in the picture and said, "All I can say is that it's destiny. How else can we explain the feeling we had from first time we met?"

Now the choice was up to us.

Do we let destiny do what's best or just remain friends. Yes of course we had a lot to talk about over the coffee that night ...

进去的照片。只是，照片中，我们两个人服饰比较怪异：我的头发盘在了头顶，表情是那么的安静祥和。我身穿立领白色的网眼长裙，长裙中间点缀着宝石。他站在我旁边，手搭在我的肩上。他穿着外套，系着领带，很帅的样子，我们看起来就是一对深爱的恋人。下一张照片中，我们的服饰都是一样的，只是这一次我们都坐着，他揽住我的腰，我斜靠在他的身边。怎么可能会这样呢，我惊讶得说不出话来，我们认识了才一周呀。每张照片几乎都和第一张照片是一样的，不同的只是照片的布景，但是照片里我们都穿着我在第一张照片中描述的那种服饰。我再也看不下去了，我抬起头来看着他的眼睛，问道："胡安，这是怎么回事？我们才认识一个星期，但是照片里的人确是我们俩，但却是某一时间的另外一种生活。"他微笑地看着我，这种微笑和照片里那位英俊的绅士看着那位女士的微笑一模一样，最后他说："我想告诉你，这就是前生注定。我们又如何解释我们初次相遇的那种感觉呢？"

现在，我们要做出自己的抉择。

我们让命运支配成为普通朋友还是彼此的另一半呢？那晚，我们喝着咖啡聊了好久……

❼ serene
/sɪˈriːn/
adj. 宁静的，平静

❽ dashing
/ˈdæʃɪŋ/
adj. 精神抖擞的，有风度的

❾ at an angel
倾斜

The best medicine
最好的药方

I knelt close to Mom to give her a hug and noticed little black hairs all over her pillow.

我跪下身来，靠近妈妈，拥抱了她，这时发现，枕头上全是一丝丝掉下来的黑头发。

Mom has always made us laugh. The only time it was hard was when the doctor said she had cancer.

"She needs an operation and strong medicine to kill the cancer," Dad said.

Mom pulled her long black hair over her shoulder. "The medicine will make my hair fall out," she said. "I might end up bald."

Nobody wanted to hear that. Mom had beautiful hair. Dad called it "black as a crow and soft as a dove."

"Maybe I will look like a bald[1] eagle," Mom added, trying to smile as she flapped[2] her arms. "Remember what the Bible says!" she reminded us. "The cheerful heart is good medicine." my sister Lucy responded.

Mom is always pulling jokes on people. Once she served Dad pancakes for breakfast. She sang rhymes[3] opera-style to call us to eat.

We didn't laugh much after Mom's operation. The medicine made her sick. She rested a lot on the couch. Every day, more of her long black hair went into the wastebasket.

It made my insides feel like knotted-up ropes to see Mom so sick. She kept trying to help us. Every night she will drill Lucy on her spelling words or math exercises.

最好的药方

妈妈经常逗我们开怀大笑,只有那一次被医生告之她患有癌症时,她笑不出来了。

"她需要做手术,需要大剂量、力量强的药来杀死癌细胞,"爸爸说。妈妈把一袭长发披在肩上。"药物会使我的头发脱落,"她说道,"最后可能变成秃顶。"

我们的真的不愿意听到这些话,妈妈有着一头乌黑、美丽的头发,爸爸称赞她的头发"像乌鸦的羽毛那样黑,像鸽子的羽毛那样柔软"。

"也许,我会变得像一只秃鹰,"妈妈补充道,她振动着双臂,试图挤出一个微笑。"想想《圣经》说过什么,"她提醒我们。"愉悦的心情是一剂良药。"我的小妹妹露西答道。

妈妈经常与人开玩笑。一次,她给爸爸做小薄饼,充当早餐,她唱着非常压韵的有如戏剧里的歌曲,叫我们来吃早餐。

妈妈手术后,我们的笑声少了很多,药物使她变得虚弱,她经常躺在沙发上,每天,都有她长长的发丝被扔进废纸篓里。

每每看到妈妈那虚弱的身体,我的内心有如打了结的绳子一样难过万分。尽管这样,她还是力所能及的要帮助我们。每天晚上,她都要帮助露西做拼读练习或是辅导她做数

❶ **bald**
/bɔːld/
n. 光秃的

❷ **flap**
/flæp/
v. 拍动

❸ **rhyme**
/raɪm/
n. 押韵

"Can I help with your homework, Tony?" Mom would ask. I always say no and go to my room. One night I just stared at my math book. I twirled[4] my pencil, watching its red-and-white-stripes turn pink and thought about Mom.

I was mad about cancer. Why should my mom get it? I missed her cooking and how she kept the house so clean. Mom used to take meals to other sick people. Now people brought meals to her.

My mattress[5] squeaked a sad tune as I lay down on my bed. On the ceiling a spider was building a web. Mom always brushed down webs. Now nobody did. Still, we were covering Mom's jobs pretty well. Dad did meals and dishes. Lucy helped with laundry[6]. I vacuumed the rugs[7]. But something important was missing in our family.

When I came home from school the next day, I didn't recognize the lady on the couch. She had Mom's eyes and smile, but she just had black fuzz on her head.

"Aunt Maria shaved my head," Mom said. "Now it won't be so messy."

I knelt close to Mom to give her a hug and noticed little black hairs all over her pillow. I pinched[8] a few between my fingers.

学练习。

"托尼，作业做得怎样，有什么问题吗？"妈妈会这样问。我经常说没有问题，然后径直地回到自己的房中。一天晚上，我盯着我的数学作业本发呆，我在手上转着铅笔，盯着铅笔的红、白条纹，慢慢的这些条纹汇成粉色，这时我又想起了妈妈。

我简直有点儿发狂了。为什么我的妈妈会得癌症？我怀念她的饭菜，怀念她把房屋打扫得那么整洁。过去，妈妈常常给别的病人送食物，而现在轮到别人给她送食物了。

躺在床上时，床垫发出了尖尖的忧郁的声响，屋顶上，一只蜘蛛正在织着网。妈妈常常清扫蜘蛛网，但现在没人扫了。我们承担起了妈妈之前做的工作，而且我们做的很不错：爸爸做饭、刷碗，露西烫洗衣服，我清扫地毯，但是，我们却缺少家庭里非常重要的东西。

第二天，下学回家，我几乎没有认出沙发上的那个女士。她有着妈妈一样的眼睛和微笑，但是头上却只有一层小绒毛。

"玛丽亚姑妈刚刚给我剃了头发，"妈妈说道："从现在开始，头发再也没那么乱了。"

我跪下身来，靠近妈妈，拥抱了她，这

❹ **twirl**
/twɜːl/
v. 旋转

❺ **mattress**
/ˈmætrɪs/
n. 床垫

❻ **laundry**
/ˈlɔːndrɪ/
n. 待洗的衣服

❼ **rug**
/rʌɡ/
n. 毛毯

❽ **pinch**
/pɪntʃ/
v. 捏

"Spider legs!" I exclaimed.

Then Mom giggled.
"Get out the spider leg eliminator!" she said.

"The what?"
"The vacuum cleaner," she whispered. "Use the hose attachment[9]."

After I vacuumed the hair off her pillow, she pointed to her head.

"Just leave some brains in there," she said. We both laughed so hard that we didn't notice Lucy coming in with the laundry basket.

"Put it here," Mom said, pointing to the floor in front of her. I started matching socks. When I looked up, Mom had put one of Dad's long socks on her arm like a puppet.

"Once upon a time there was a mom with cancer," she made the sock puppet say. "She didn't have bad hair days. She had no-hair days."

Mom looked at me. I knew she wanted me to make a joke, too. But I didn't want to make fun of her losing her hair.

时发现,枕头上全是一丝丝掉下来的黑头发。我捡起一些发丝,在指间揉捏。

"蜘蛛腿!"我大叫着。

然后,妈妈笑了。

"去拿清扫蜘蛛腿的机器,"她说道。

"拿什么?"

"吸尘器,"她低语道,"用那个软管。"

把头发吸干净后,她指着她的脑袋。

"只剩下智慧了,"她说道。我们俩笑起来。我们没有注意到露西拿着洗衣篮进来了。

"放在这儿吧,"妈妈说,指着她面前的地板。

我开始把袜子按对配好。当我抬起头时,我看到妈妈把爸爸的其中一个长袜套在她的胳膊上,有如一个木偶。

"从前,有这样一位妈妈,她患了癌症,"她给这个用袜子做的木偶配着音,"她不再拥有令人烦恼的、不顺滑的头发,却开始了没有头发的时代。"

妈妈看着我,我知道她想让我也开个玩笑,但是我不想以她脱发开玩笑。

"轮到你了,"她坚持道。

⑨ attachment
/əˈtætʃmənt/
n. 附加装置

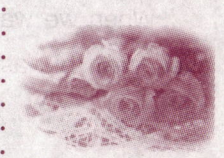

"Your turn," she insisted.

I pulled on another sock and had it reply in a squeaky[10] voice, "My name is Billy Bald. I comb my hair with a wash cloth."

Even Lucy made a puppet with one of her fuzzy[11] socks.

"I am Fuzzy Lucy," she had her puppet say. "Life is hairy around here."

Mom kept laughing as we made up a story for a few minutes. Finally, she said, "That is enough. Please put the laundry away." Then she lay back down to sleep.

As I put my socks in a drawer, I looked in my dresser mirror. I had hair like Mom's, black and wavy. Whenever I went to the barber, she always said, "Don't let him cut too much off." Just then I got an idea that Dad would have to help me.

"We will head to the barber," Dad told Mom the next Saturday morning.

"Don't let him take too much off," she said, like always.

When we walked in the door a couple hours later, Mom's eyes grew big as chocolate candies. "I don't believe it!" Mom said.

我在手上套上另一支袜子，尖声尖气地说："我的名字叫秃头比利。我每天用湿布梳头发。"

露西也用她的毛绒绒的袜子做了个木偶。

"我是茸茸露西，"她给木偶配着音，"我们周围的生活是毛茸茸的，到处都是毛发。"

我们又编了几分钟的故事，妈妈被逗得一直在笑。最后，她说道："好了好了，把衣服放好吧。"然后，她躺在沙发上又睡了。

我把袜子放进了抽屉，我看了看穿衣镜中的自己。我有着和妈妈一样的又浓又黑的头发。每次我去理发店，她都会说"不要剪得太多"。这时我有了一个想法，而且爸爸一定会支持我。

"我们要去理发店，"星期六的早上，爸爸对妈妈这样说道。

"别剪太多，"像平时一样她这样说道。

几小时后，我们进屋时，妈妈惊诧地把眼睛睁得像巧克力糖那样大。"我简直不敢相信我的眼睛！"

妈妈说道。

"我也是，"露西补充道。

"看看，现在我们三个人多协调呀，"我笑着说。因为，我和爸爸都把头剃光了。

10 squeaky
/ˈskwiːkɪ/
adj. 尖叫声的

11 fuzzy
/ˈfʌzɪ/
adj. 毛茸茸的

"Neither do I," added Lucy.

"Now three of us match," I said with a big grin[12]. Dad and I had asked the barber to shave us bald.

"I have shaved," I said in a high puppet voice that got Mom laughing again. "I comb my hair with a wash cloth."

"It will grow again," Mom said as she rubbed[13] my bare head.

"You are so funny," Lucy said. "I am getting the camera."

You knew where I would put the photo: in the Family Funny.

最好的药方

"我把头剃光了。"我尖尖地模仿木偶的声音说道,这下把妈妈逗乐了。"我用湿布梳头发。"

"头发还会长起来的,"妈妈边抚摸着我的光头边说。

"你太有意思了,"露西说道,"我去拿相机。"

知道我的照片被放在哪了吗,放在家里的《欢喜家庭》的影集里了。

12 grin
/grɪn/
n. 露齿的笑

13 rub
/'rʌb/
v. 揉揉

Is it worth the risk?
值得冒险吗?

But I realized that at the end of my life, the car would have no value and neither would the house. The only things that had steadfast value were experiences.

然而,生命终结的时候,汽车和房子其实没有任何价值;惟一恒久不变的价值是你的体验和经历。

情 感 篇

A number of years ago (1983—1987), I had the opportunity to play the character of Ronald McDonald for the McDonald's Corporation.

One of our standard events was "Ronald Day." One day each month, we visited as many of the community hospitals as possible, bringing a little happiness into a place where no one ever looks forward to going. I was very proud to be able to make a difference for children and adults who were experiencing some "down time." The warmth and gratification[1] I would receive stayed with me for weeks. I loved the project, McDonald's loved the project, the kids and adults loved it and so did the nursing and hospital staffs.

There were two restrictions placed on me during a visit. First, I could not go anywhere in the hospital without McDonald's personnel as well as hospital personnel. And second, I could not physically touch anyone within the hospital. They did not want me transferring germs from one patient to another. I understood why they had this "don't touch" rule, but I didn't like it. I believe that touching is the most honest form of communication we will ever know. Printed and spoken words can lie; it is impossible to lie with a warm hug.

Breaking either of these rules, I was told, meant I could lose my job. One day, as I was heading down a hallway after a long day in grease paint[2] and on my way home, I heard a little voice. "Ronald, Ronald."

值得冒险吗?

几年前（1983—1987），我有幸在麦当劳公司扮演罗纳德·麦当劳。

其中一个标准的活动便是"罗纳节"。每个月我们都会抽出一天，去探望那些没人问津的社区医院，把祝福和笑声带给他们。对此，我很是自豪，因为我能给那些身处不幸的大人和孩子送上我们与众不同的东西。他们给予我的热情和感激会陪伴我好几周。我以及麦当劳公司的员工喜欢这个活动，大人、孩子以及和医院的医护人员也喜欢这个活动。

对医院的探访活动有两个限制条件。第一，没有麦当劳公司以及医护人员的陪同，我不能到处走动。第二，我不能与任何人有任何身体接触，因为他们不想由此造成病菌传染。我明白为什么他们有"不许接触"这个原则，但是我不喜欢，我觉得接触是交流中最可信的方式。书写和口头表达都有自己的虚伪性，然而一个热情的拥抱不会掺杂任何的虚假。

我被告之如果违反任何一条规则都将被炒鱿鱼。那天，忙了一天，披了一天的化妆油彩，我从大厅走下来，准备回家，这时我听到了一个柔柔的声音，"罗纳德，罗纳德"。

❶ gratification
/ˌɡrætɪfɪˈkeɪʃən/
n. 感谢,感激

❷ grease paint
化妆油彩

I stopped. The soft little voice was coming through a half-opened door. I pushed the door open and saw a young boy, about five years old, lying in his dad's arms, hooked[3] up to more medical equipment than I had ever seen. Mom was on the other side, along with Grandma, Grandpa and a nurse tending to the equipment.

I knew by the feeling in the room that the situation was grave. I asked the little boy his name. He told me it was Billy and I did a few simple magic tricks for him. As I stepped back to say goodbye, I asked Billy if there was anything else I could do for him.

"Ronald, would you hold me?"

Such a simple request[4]. But what ran through my mind was that if I touched him, I could lose my job. So I told Billy I could not do that right now, but I suggested that he and I color a picture. Upon completing a wonderful piece of art that we were both very proud of, Billy again asked me to hold him. By this time my heart was screaming, "Yes!" But my mind was screaming louder, "No! You are going to lose your job!"

This second time that Billy asked me, I had to ponder[5] why I could not grant the simple request of a little boy who probably would not be going home. I asked myself why was I being logically and emotionally torn apart by someone I had never seen before and probably would never see again.

我停下来，发现声音是从一个房门半开着的房间传出来的。我推开门，看到一个浑身挂着医疗器械的五岁男孩，正躺在他父亲的臂弯里。我真的没见过浑身吊着这么多医疗器械的人。他的父亲、母亲、外公、外婆都在病房，屋里还有一个正对着器械的护士。

凭感觉我知道这里的情势很不好。我问了孩子的名字，他告诉我他叫比利，然后我给他表演了几个简单的小魔术。当我和他说告别时，我问小比利还有什么我可以做的。

"罗纳德，你可以抱抱我吗？"

多么简单的请求呀，但是我突然想到，如果抱了他，我会失去工作。我对比利说现在不能抱他，但是我说我可以和他一起画画。画完一幅我们都引以为豪的"作品"后，比利又一次让我抱抱他。这一次，我的内心在呐喊："抱抱他吧"，但是我的思维在大声喊道："不行，你会丢掉工作的！"

这次，我在思考为什么我不能满足这个孩子的要求呢，也许他再也不能回家了。我问自己为什么我的情感和思维被这个过去未曾谋面，以后可能永远都不会见到的人所搅动。

❸ **hook**
/huk/
v. 钩，钩住

❹ **request**
/rɪˈkwest/
n. 要求，恳求

❺ **ponder**
/ˈpɒndə/
v. 沉思，考虑

情 感 篇

"Hold me." It was such a simple request, and yet I searched for any reasonable response that would allow me to leave. I could not come up with[6] a single one. It took me a moment to realize that in this situation, losing my job may not be the disaster I feared.

Was losing my job the worst thing in the world?

Did I have enough self-belief that if I did lose my job, I would be able to pick up and start again? The answer was a loud, bold affirming "yes!" I could pick up and start again.

So what was the risk?

Just that if I lost my job, it probably would not be long before I would lose first my car, then my home, and to be honest with you, I really liked those things. But I realized that at the end of my life, the car would have no value and neither would the house. The only things that had steadfast value were experiences. Once I reminded myself that the real reason I was there was to bring a little happiness to an unhappy environment, I realized that I really faced no risk at all.

I sent Mom, Dad, Grandma and Grandpa out of the room, and my two McDonald's escorts out to the van[7]. The nurse tending the medical equipment stayed, but Billy asked her to stand and face the corner. Then, I picked up this little wonder of a human being. He was so frail and so scared. We laughed and cried for 45 minutes and talked about the things that worried him.

"抱抱我",多么简单的请求呀,然而我却不能满足他。我搜寻着能够离开这里的合理理由,但是一个也找不出来,这个时候我突然觉得,失去工作也不会像灾难那么的可怕。

失去工作是世界上最可怕、最糟糕的事情吗?

如果丢掉这份工作,我还可以再找一份,重新开始吗?回答是大声的、肯定的,"是的"我可以重新开始一份新的工作。

那么存在的风险又是什么呢?

如果丢了这份工作,首先车就会没有了,然后是房子,说实话,我真的很喜欢这些东西。然而,生命终结的时候,汽车和房子其实没有任何价值;惟一恒久不变的价值是你的体验和经历。当想起来这里的目的是给他们送来欢乐时,我意识到其实我根本没有风险。

我把他的爸爸、妈妈、外公、外婆送出屋去,把麦当劳的两个陪同人员打发到大车上,对着医疗器械的护士还在,比利叫她站起来,面对着墙脚。然后,我抱起了这个小古怪,他是那么虚弱又是那么慌张,我们笑着叫着足有45分钟,我和他一起谈着他所担忧的事。

❻ come up with
找到或提出(答案、办法等)

❼ van
/væn/
n. 大车,大蓬车

Billy was afraid that his little brother might get lost coming home from kindergarten next year, without Billy to show him the way. He worried that his dog wouldn't get another bone because Billy had hidden the bones in the house before going back to the hospital and now he couldn't remember where he put them.

These are problems to a little boy who knows he isn't going home.

On my way of the room, with tears in my eyes, I gave Mom and Dad my real name and phone number and said if there was anything the McDonald's Corporation or I could do, to give me a call and consider it done.

Less than 48 hours later, I received a phone call from Billy's mom. She informed me that Billy had passed away. She and her husband simply wanted to thank me for making a difference in their little boy's life.

Billy's mom told me that shortly after I left the room, Billy looked at her and said, "Momma, I don't care anymore if I see Santa this year because I was held by Ronald McDonald."

For the record, McDonald's did find out about Billy and me, but given the circumstances[8], permitted me to retain[9] my job. I continued as Ronald for another year before leaving the corporation to share the story of Billy and how important it is to take risks.

值得冒险吗？

比利担心明年没有他带路，小弟弟会找不着回家的路。他担心他的狗找不到骨头吃，住院前，他把骨头藏在家里了，但是他现在想不起藏哪儿了。

这就是一个自知再也回不了家的孩子所担心的问题。

我噙着泪水，离开了病房。我把我的真实姓名和电话号码告诉了那位父亲和那位母亲，对他们说，如果需要我和麦当劳公司的帮忙，就给我打电话。

48小时还没有到，比利的母亲给我打来了电话，她告诉我比利永远的离开了。她和她丈夫只是想向我道声感谢，因为是我让他们的孩子在生命的最后时刻感到了幸福。

比利的母亲告诉我，我走后不久，比利看着她说："妈咪，我不介意今年是否能看到圣诞老人了，因为罗纳德·麦当劳抱了我。"

后来，公司还是发现了我抱了比利这件事，但是考虑到当时的情况，他们没把我辞掉。因此，我又干了一年扮演罗纳德的工作。之后，我离开麦当劳公司，把比利的故事讲给别人听，告诉他们冒险是多么的重要。

8 circumstance
/ˈsɜːkəmstəns/
n. 环境，事件

9 retain
/rɪˈteɪn/
v. 保持，留有

A peculiar yet familiar feeling
一种特别又熟悉的感觉

A peculiar yet familiar feeling came upon me today when I walked outdoors to retrieve my mail.

今天,当我走出房门去取邮件时,一种奇特但非常熟悉的感觉向我袭来。

A peculiar yet familiar feeling came upon me today when I walked outdoors to retrieve[1] my mail ... I actually got very excited about it!

I was feeling the same exhilarating[2] high I used to get when I would sign on-line and have e-mail. I must admit though, I felt somewhat ashamed that I had almost lost touch with the off-line world out there.

E-mail can never beat the heartfelt thoughts and well wishes that go into a handwritten note from a dear friend. I can't remember ever receiving a letter from someone special where I could possibly misinterpret EXACTLY what was hand written!

I've had plenty of opportunity to go back and forth with various e-pals because I didn't quite understand the inflection[3] in their type-written notes to me or misconstrued[4] the meaning behind their/my grins, "!" remarks. Many times I have continued on in jest[5] only to find out later that they were never kidding, or I found out that my remarks were "believed" and someone missed the "just kidding" from me!

I hope we all never get so net-involved that we lose touch with our ability to make someone's day by writing a few special words on paper and dropping it into the mail.

In spite of postage increases, mail is still cheap! Can you imagine a life without ever receiving a greeting card in the mail?

一种特别又熟悉的感觉

今天,当我走出房门去取邮件时,一种奇特但非常熟悉的感觉向我袭来。事实上,拿到这封信我激动万分!

其实,当我在网上冲浪并且收到 E-mail 时,我有着和现在收取信件一样的欢快、激动之情,但是我必须承认,我真的很羞愧,因为我几乎与网络之外的现实世界隔绝了。

E-mail 永远不及亲密的朋友手写来的信件诚挚。我几乎记不起来收到过来信,甚至写"EXACTLY"我都有可能拼错。

我常常不太固定地与许多的网友聊过,因为有的时候我不太理解他们敲给我的一些符号和表情,有的时候可能会误解一个笑脸或叹号的含意。许多次,我半开玩笑地与他们聊天,最后发现他们并没欺骗我,他们也很信我的话。有些人非常怀念我在网上常说的"骗骗人"。

我希望我们不要这么沉迷于网络,因为这样的话,我们将会失去写下一段特别的话寄给某人来愉悦他的能力。

尽管邮资在上涨,寄封信其实还是很便宜的。你能想像收不到贺卡的生活吗?

❶ retrieve
/rɪ'tiːv/
v. 找回,取回

❷ exhilarating
/ɪɡ'zɪləreɪtɪŋ/
adj. 使人高兴的

❸ inflection
/ɪn'flekʃən/
n. 变形,变化

❹ misconstrue
/ˈmɪskənˈstruː/
v. 误会,误解

❺ in jest
开玩笑地

I actually e-mailed a few "dads" I knew on Father's Day and wished them a special day. In hindsight[6], I can only imagine the joy they might have felt, had I taken the time to select that special card among thousands and mailed a card to them.

There are cyber-flower services out there on the world wide web! Personally, I'd hate to imagine the day I no longer receive REAL flowers ... one's that I can actually enjoy the aroma ...

I think I'll spend some time tonight writing something special to those forgotten few who have not yet experienced the wonderful and sometimes impersonal cyber-world out there.

父亲节那天，我认识了许多新"爸爸"，我把我的祝愿以 E-mail 形式送给了他们，事后我能想像得到当他们知道我在成百上千的贺卡中选择这样一个特殊卡片寄给他们时，他们会多么快乐。

互联网上也有送虚拟鲜花的服务，但是对我个人来讲，我可不喜欢再也收不到真正鲜花的那一天。我喜欢那种散发着花香的真正鲜花。

今天晚上，我应该花些时间给那些被遗忘的人写点儿特别的东西，那些没有体验过如此精彩、有时缺点儿人情味的虚拟网络中的人。

❻ **hindsight**
/ˈhaɪndsaɪt/
n. 事后的认识

My mother
我的妈妈

MaWee wasn't perfect. But she loved me perfectly.
I am proud to say that I am my mother's daughter.

MaWee 并不完美,但她近乎完美地爱着我。
我非常自豪地说我是我母亲的女儿。

While a toddler, I can remember MaWee bailing[1] me out of a hopeless situation. I was playing with my doll's hot water bottle, and when it bounced[2] under an overstuffed chair, I was unable to reach it. I cried out in frustration and MaWee came to my rescue. She tilted the chair way back and retrieved[3] it for me. As a 2-3 year old, I can remember to this day, how strong she was to lift the chair and give me back my toy.

At 4.5 years old, I remember how she cared for me while I was experiencing the excruciating[4] pain of a ruptured appendix[5]. She drove me to the hospital herself. After the surgery, I remember how she lovingly taught me, because I wasn't supposed to show EVERYBODY my scar!

She taught me culture; I took ballet, acrobatic and tap dancing lessons. I remember her support of me the night I danced to "Dance with the Dolly with a Hole in Her Stocking" at a talent night with the dance studio.

It was MaWee who handmade my mouse outfit for a number I did for ballet, and my outfit was complete with *PINK* ears! I was the *ONLY* mouse with pink ears! It was MaWee who wanted me to ... stand out in a crowd!

She gave me opportunities to learn piano and let me take skating rink lessons. It was MaWee who taught me that "pretty is as pretty does". She said many times, "If you can't say something nice about someone, it's best not to say anything at all."

我的妈妈

记得刚刚学会走路时，MaWee 常常会在我需要帮助的时候，把我从"困境"中救出。一天我正在玩一个布娃娃的热水壶，不小心，它却弹到了椅子下，椅子下塞得满满的全都是东西，我根本够不着。我沮丧地大声叫嚷，是 MaWee 这时过来帮助了我。她把椅子向后挪了挪，把水壶取出来了。直到现在我都记得那一切。对于一个两三岁的孩子来说，她是那么有力，能够举起椅子帮我把玩具捡回来。

4岁半的时候，我做了一次阑尾穿孔手术，那次疼极了，现在我还记得当时的情景，她是那么精心的照顾我，而且是她亲自把我送到医院的。手术后，她充满慈爱的开导我，因为，我不想让任何人看到我的伤疤。

她教我各式各样的文化；我参加了芭蕾、杂技和踢踏舞的活动班。我仍记得那个令人难忘的，在舞蹈演播室度过的那个夜晚。那天我跳了舞名为《与长袜上有个洞洞的多利跳舞》，那天她给了我许多帮助。

MaWee 为我亲手做了一套米老鼠的衣服，这套衣服是我跳芭蕾舞时要用的，这套米老鼠服装有着粉色耳朵。我是惟一一名穿着有着粉色耳朵的米老鼠服装的，因为 MaWee 想让我在众多的小朋友中脱颖而出。

她使我有机会学习了钢琴、接触到了滑

❶ bail
/beɪl/
v. 脱困

❷ bounce
/baʊns/
v. 弹起，反弹

❸ retrieve
/rɪˈtriːv/
v. 找回

❹ excruciating
/ɪkˈskruːʃieɪtɪŋ/
adj. 极痛苦的

❺ ruptured appendix
阑尾穿孔手术

She taught me to think before I speak.

MaWee taught me to be frugal; she showed me how to save money. In fact, I had so much saved back that I played store with my real money. I can remember MaWee and Dad, borrowing money from me when they wanted to go to the movies before payday. She also must have taught me about interest[6] ... so I always got back a little more than I had given. ;—)

At the dinner table in 5th grade, I casually mentioned that I'd learned "how you make babies" from my friends at school. It was Ma Wee, who took the time after dinner to teach me the more appropriate facts of life.

When MaWee remarried, I was experiencing quite a bit of jealous[7] feelings, going from the baby of the family to the oldest, with 3 younger stepsiblings. It was MaWee who woke me up before the rest of the family, just so we could have quiet time alone together.

It was MaWee who gave me my first "physical attribute" compliment. Back in the late sixties, we wore micro-mini skirts to high school. MaWee had picked me up from school and told she watched me cross the street and had noticed how "cute" my legs looked in my mini skirt. Gee, they looked just like hers ... no wonder!!

It was MaWee who trusted my judgment enough to allow me

冰，是妈妈教会我"行动美，才会显得美。"她曾多次对我说，"如果你不想说别人的好话，那最好就什么也不要说"。她教会了我开口之前，要先动脑筋去思考。

MaWee 教育我要节俭，她教我如何攒钱。事实上，我存了一些钱，我记得爸爸、妈妈曾经向我借过钱，因为那时他们想去看电影，但是还没有领到工资。她还教我怎样去获得利息……因此我经常能够领到比所存钱数更多的数额。

五年级的时候，一次在餐桌上，我向妈妈提到了我从同学那儿学到的"你是怎么生小孩儿"这件事。是 MaWee 第一次告诉了我生命中一些确切的事情。

MaWee 再婚了，我真的有一点儿嫉妒。按年龄排，我有了3个同母异父的弟妹。在家里的其他人还没有醒来前，MaWee 把我叫醒，为了能和我单独相处一会儿。

是 MaWee 第一次称赞我"性感"。60年代末，我在上高中，那时都穿迷你裙去上学。下学后，妈妈来接我，她告诉我当我穿过大街时，她注意到我的大腿在迷你裙的衬托下是那么迷人。哈，当然我的腿像她的一样漂亮！

MaWee 相信我的眼光，允许我与一名男孩去看电影，那可是我的第一次约会啊！

6 **interest**
/ˈɪntrɪst/
n. 利息

7 **jealous**
/ˈdʒeləs/
adj. 妒忌的

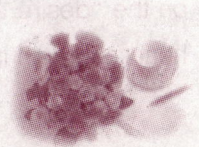

to go to a drive-in movie ... with a boy ... on a *FIRST* date!

MaWee was there to comfort me when I got dumped[8] by a boyfriend and I thought I'd never <u>get over</u>[9] him. She told me there were plenty of "fish" in the sea. She told me I'd one day find God's best for me, a man who wouldn't hurt me like this boy had. Years later, when I went through the heartbreak of a divorce, it was MaWee who cried with me over long distance calls.

MaWee showed respect to the men of my life, even when she didn't approve. She was also there for me when the relationships went sour. She shared from her heart, and taught me how to move on.

MaWee has loved my own children by her actions. She's made "memories in the mail" so that they knew who Grandma was, even while she was living out of state. It was her way of influencing their lives. She sent many a Christian tract, wholesome[10] articles and magazines. To this day, my children look forward to hearing from her in this way.

Growing up, I have many fond memories of beaches, parks, picnics and hunting trips with Dad, of spending time with my grandparents, of many different church outings. MaWee passed on the "desire to write" and taught me by example how to put my heart and soul into words. It is now my favorite pastime[11].

当我被男友抛弃，并且自认为无法忘记他时，MaWee安慰我说天下男孩多的是，我应该去找一个更好的，找一个永远都不会像这个男孩一样伤害我的好男人。许多年后，当我结束了一段令人心碎的婚姻后，MaWee给我打了长途电话，她在电话的那一头，与我哭在了一起。

MaWee对我生活中的男人都很尊敬，尽管她有时不赞成我和有些人来往。当我和他们之间的关系变坏时，MaWee会一直在身边陪伴我，告诉我如何继续前进。

MaWee以行动关爱我的孩子，她做了一个"信件回忆录"，以便让我的孩子知道谁是他们的外祖母，即使她不在人世了，孩子们也能记住他。她以她自己的方式影响着孩子们的生活，她给他们寄圣诞小册子，给他们寄一些健康的文章和杂志，直到现在，我的孩子们都盼望着收到她的信件。

长大成人后，我会常常回忆起在海滩、公园、野餐时的那些美丽时光，会经常回忆起与爸爸狩猎的事情，会回忆起与外婆在一起的时光，也会回忆起那种类繁多的教堂远足。MaWee把她的"写作欲"灌输给我，并且身体力行的教我如何把内心的感情转化为笔下的文字。现在，写作已成为我最大的爱好。

⑧ **dump**
/dʌmp/
v. 抛弃

⑨ **get over**
把…忘怀

⑩ **wholesome**
/ˈhəulsəm/
adj. 健康的

⑪ **pastime**
/ˈpɑːstaɪm/
n. 娱乐

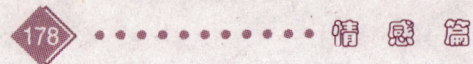

MaWee wasn't perfect. But she loved me perfectly. As you've seen, MaWee got to see me in good times and bad ... but she's always stood by me and loved me unconditionally[12]. I am proud to say that I am my mother's daughter.

我的妈妈

MaWee 并不完美，但她近乎完美地爱着我。就像你所看到的那样，无论我处在什么状态，高兴也好，难过也罢，她都会站在我的身边，给予我支持，无条件的爱着我。我非常自豪地说我是我母亲的女儿。

⑫ **unconditionally**
/ˌʌnkənˈdɪʃənəlɪ/
adv. 无条件地

The color of friendship
友谊的色彩

The colors crouched down in fear, drawing close to one another for comfort.

各种颜色恐惧地蹲下身来,紧凑在一起寻求安慰。

Once upon a time the colors of the world started to quarrel. All claimed that they were the best. The most important. The most useful. The most beautiful. The favorite.

Green said:

"Clearly I am the most important. I am the sign of life and of hope. I was chosen for grass, trees and leaves. Without me, all animals would die. Look over the countryside and you will see that I am in the majority."

Blue interrupted:

"You only think about the earth, but consider the sky and the sea. It is the water that is the basis of life and drawn up by the clouds from the deep sea. The sky gives space and peace and serenity. Without my peace, you would all be nothing."

Yellow chuckled[1]:

"You are all so serious. I bring laughter, gaiety[2], and warmth into the world. The sun is yellow, the moon is yellow, and the stars are yellow. Every time you look at a sunflower, the whole world starts to smile. Without me there would be no fun."

Orange started next to <u>blow her trumpet</u>[3]:

"I am the color of health and strength. I may be scarce, but I am precious for I serve the needs of human life. I carry the most important vitamins. Think of carrots, pumpkins, oranges, mangoes, and papayas. I don't hang around all the time, but when I fill the sky at sunrise or sunset, my beauty is so striking that no

友谊的色彩

很久很久以前，世界上的各种颜色开始争吵起来，每种颜色都宣称自己最棒、最重要、最有用、最漂亮、最惹人喜爱。

绿色说道：

"很明显，我最重要，因为我象征着生命和希望。小草、大树以及树叶都是绿色的。没有我，所有的动物都不能存活，看看我们的大地吧，绿色简直就是统治色。"

蓝色打断它说道：

"你只看到了大地，看看天空和海洋吧。水是生命的基本组成部分，水由海水蒸发凝成云团降雨形成。天空是那么广阔、平和、安宁，没有象征着和平的蓝色，你们将什么都不是。"

黄色笑道：

"你们都太严肃了，只有我会给世界带来笑声、愉快和温暖。太阳是黄色的，月亮是黄色的，星星也是黄色的。每当你看太阳花时，全世界都在向你微笑，没有我，世界就没有欢乐。"

桔色开始自吹自擂起来：

"桔色代表着健康和力量。我的颜色比较罕见，但是由于提供人类生命所需要的物质，因而显得异常珍贵。我的颜色携带很多重要的维他命，想想胡萝卜、南瓜、桔子、芒果、和木瓜吧，它们都是桔色。我并不是天天出现，但是日出或日落时，我将天空镶上一层

❶ chuckle
/ˈtʃʌkl/
v. 暗自笑

❷ gaiety
/ˈɡeɪəti/
n. 欢乐，华丽

❸ blow one's trumpet
自吹自擂

one gives another thought to any of you."

Red could stand it no longer he shouted out:
"I am the ruler of all of you. I am blood — life's blood! I am the color of danger and of bravery. I am willing to fight for a cause. I bring fire into the blood. Without me, the earth would be as empty as the moon. I am the color of passion and of love, the red rose, the poinsettia and the poppy."

Purple rose up to his full height, he was very tall and spoke with great pomp[4]:
"I am the color of royalty and power. Kings, chiefs, and bishops have always chosen me for I am the sign of authority and wisdom. People do not question me! They listen and obey."

Finally Indigo[5] spoke, much more quietly than all the others, but with just as much determination: "Think of me. I am the color of silence. You hardly notice me, but without me you all become superficial. I represent thought and reflection, twilight and deep water. You need me for balance and contrast, for prayer and inner peace."

And so the colors went on boasting, each convinced of his or her own superiority[6]. Their quarreling became louder and louder. Suddenly there was a startling flash of bright lightening, thunder rolled and boomed. Rain started to pour down relentlessly. The colors crouched down in fear, drawing close to one another for comfort.

漂亮无比的颜色，你们都将显得逊色许多，没人会想到你们。"

红色再也不能忍受了，它喊道：

"我是你们的统治者，我是血，生命的颜色！我象征着危险和勇敢，我愿为事业而奋战。我把火种带到了我们的世界。没有我，地球将像月球那样光秃一片。红色代表着激情和爱情，它也是红玫瑰、一品红和罂粟的颜色。"

紫色站起来，他非常高大，说起话来气势磅礴：

"我象征着皇室和权力，国王、领袖、主教选我们为他们的代表色，因为我象征着权力和智慧。人们不会怀疑我，他们听从、服从我。"

较之其他几种颜色，靛蓝色说话平和许多，但是同样富有决心：

"想想我吧，我是安静的象征。你们很少注意到我，但是没有我，你们都将沦为肤浅。我象征着思考和沉思，象征着曙光和一池深水。我的作用是使你们的颜色保持协调，形成对比，你们需要我来祈祷和保持心灵的平和。"

颜色之间还在互相吹嘘，夸捧着自己比其他颜色好，他们的争吵声越来越大。突然，一道闪光从天空划过，雷声慢慢袭来，雨猛烈地下了起来。各种颜色恐惧地蹲下身来，

❹ **pomp**
/pɒmp/
n. 华丽，盛况

❺ **indigo**
/ˈɪndɪɡəʊ/
n. 靛蓝

❻ **superiority**
/sjuːpɪərɪˈɒrɪti/
n. 优越性，优势

In the midst of the clamor[7], rain began to speak:

"You foolish colors, fighting amongst yourselves, each trying to dominate the rest. Don't you know that you were each made for a special purpose, unique and different? Join hands with one another and come to me."

Doing as they were told, the colors united and joined hands.

The rain continued:

"From now on, when it rains, each of you will stretch across the sky in a great bow of color as a reminder that you can all live in peace. The Rainbow is a sign of hope for tomorrow." And so, whenever a good rain washes the world, and a Rainbow appears in the sky, to let us remember to appreciate one another.

友谊的色彩

紧凑在一起寻求安慰。

喧闹声中，雨开始说道：

"你们是多么愚蠢呀，竟然互相攻击，试图去统治别人。难道你们不知道你们每种颜色都有自己的特定的用处吗？你们各自都独特、与众不同。现在，你们手拉手一块到这儿来。"

按照雨的指示，颜色们手拉手团结起来向雨走过去。

雨继续说道：

"从现在开始，只要一下雨，你们每种颜色都要加入到天空的彩虹中去，彩虹代表着你们颜色间的和平相处。彩虹是明天希望的象征。"因此，每当一场及时雨清洗了我们的世界后，天空便会横挂一条彩虹，那时，让我们记住去欣赏他们的每一种颜色。

7 clamor

/ˈklæmə/

n. 喧闹，吵闹

The secret of happiness
幸福的奥秘

I've already adapted. Now you also have to get used to this.

我已经适应了这一切,这一次轮到你们来适应我只剩下一条腿的境况。

A young man once came to meet me in Jerusalem. He had an unusually happy disposition[1], so I asked him what's his secret. He told me:

"When I was 11 years old, I received a gift of happiness from God."

"I was riding my bicycle when a strong gust[3] of wind blew me onto the ground into the path of an oncoming truck. The truck ran over me and cut off my leg."

"As I lay there bleeding, I realized that I might have to live the rest of my life without a leg. How depressing! But then I realized that being depressed[2] won't get my leg back. So I decided right then and there not to waste my life despairing."

"When my parents arrived at the hospital they were shocked and grieving[3]. So I told them: 'I've already adapted. Now you also have to get used to this.'"

"Ever since then, I see my friends getting upset over little things: their bus came late, they got a bad grade on a test, somebody insulted[9] them. But I just enjoy life."

At age 11, this young man attained the clarity[4] that it is a waste of energy to focus on what you are missing. And that the key to happiness is to take pleasure in what you have.

我曾经在耶路撒冷遇到这样一个年轻人，他有着非同寻常的快乐性格，因此，我问他他快乐的秘密是什么，他对我说：

"11岁的时候，我意外地收到了一样东西。"

"那天，我在街上骑着自行车，一阵大风把我吹到街中央，这时迎面驶来一辆大货车，把我撞倒在地，轧伤了我的一条腿。"

"血不断地流，那时我意识到，我的下半生将会在只有一条腿的情况下度过，当时我沮丧万分，但是，我很快意识到悲伤沮丧都无法换回失去的那条腿，因此，我决定，以后决不能把时间浪费在悲伤、难过中。"

"我父母赶到医院时，他们既惊愕又难过，我对他们说：'我已经适应了这一切，这一次轮到你们来适应我只剩下一条腿的境况。'"

"从此以后，看到我的朋友们因一些小事，比如：汽车晚点，考试失利，有人对他们出言不逊等等而难过、沮丧时，我都会笑对人生、享受生活。"

这个年轻人在11岁时，就已经明白了把时间和精力用在已经失去的事物上是一种浪费，而快乐、幸福的秘密就是享受并珍惜现在拥有的。

❶ disposition
/ˌdɪspəˈzɪʃən/
n. 性情，性格

❷ depressed
/dɪˈprest/
adj. 使沮丧

❸ grieve
/ɡriːv/
v. 悲痛，伤心

❹ clarity
/ˈklærɪtɪ/
n. 明晰

To feel better, you need to think better
心之所想，行之所依

Like it or not, you travel through life with your thoughts spell gloom and doom, that's where you're headed.

无论你信不信，这种悲观和忧郁的思想都会伴随你一生，这就是你必须面对的。

情感篇

It's the classic story with a twist: a traveling salesman gets a flat tire on a dark, lonely road and then discovers he has no jack[1]. He sees a light in a farmhouse. As he walks toward it, his mind churns: "Suppose no one comes to the door." "Suppose they don't have a jack." "Suppose the guy won't lend me his jack even if he has one." The harder his mind works, the more agitated[2] he becomes, and when the door opens, he punches the farmer and said yells, "Keep your lousy jack!"

That story brings a smile, because it pokes fun at a common type of self-defeatist thinking. How often have you heard yourself say: "Nothing ever goes the way I planned." "I'll never make that deadline." "I always screw up."

Such inner speech shapes your life more than any other single force. Like it or not, you travel through life with your thoughts spell gloom and doom, that's where you're headed, because put-down words sabotage[3] confidence instead of offering support and encouragement.

Simply put, to feel better, you need to think better. Here's how:

1. *Tune into your thoughts.* The first thing Sue said to her new therapist was, "I know you can't help me, Doctor. I'm a total mess. I keep lousing up at work, and I'm sure I'm going to be canned. Just yesterday my boss told me I was being transferred. He called it promotion. But if I was doing

这是一个经典的故事。一个有些怪诞的销售员在旅途中一处极黑暗冷清的地方抛锚了。而且他发现没有带千斤顶。这时，他看到一个农舍里透出灯光，便朝那里走过去。一边走，一边忐忑不安地想"如果没人来开门怎么办？"一会儿又想"要是他们没有千斤顶，或者即使有也不借给我又怎么办？"越想越不安，当门打开时，他一拳击中开门的农夫，并大吼道："收起你那个该死的千斤顶吧。"

这个故事听起来很好笑，他是对那种自我挫败的想法的讽刺。你有多少次自己对自己说："没有一件事是按计划进行的。""我决不可能按时完成。""我总是搞砸。"

这种内在的想法比任何一种外来的压力更能影响你的生活。无论你信不信，这种悲观和忧郁的思想都会伴随你一生，这就是你必须面对的，因为贬低的话语只会毁掉你的信心而决不可能带来支持和鼓励。

简而言之要想感到称心如意就必须先往好的方向去想。以下是几点建议：

1. 调整你的思想。苏对她的新的心理医生说的第一句话就是："我知道你帮不了我，医生，我总是一团糟。我的工作一直都有问题，我就要被解雇了。就在昨天我的老板告

❶ jack
/dʒæk/
n. 千斤顶

❷ agitated
/ˈædʒɪteɪtɪd/
adj. 焦虑的

❸ sabotage
/ˈsæbətɑːʒ/
v. 破坏

a good job, why transfer me?"

Then, gradually, Sue's story moved past the put-downs. She had received her M.B.A. two years before and was making an excellent salary. That didn't sound like failure.

At the end of their first meeting, Sue's therapist told her to jot down her thoughts, particularly at night if she was having trouble falling asleep. At her next appointment Sue's list included: "I'm not really smart. I got ahead by a bunch of flukes." "Tomorrow will be a disaster. I've never chaired a meeting before." "My boss looked furious this morning. What did I do?"

She admitted, "In one day alone, I listed 26 negative thoughts. No wonder I'm always tired and depressed."

Hearing her fears and forebodings read out loud made Sue realize how much energy she was squandering[4] on imagined catastrophes[5]. If you've been feeling down, it could be you're sending yourself negative message too. Listen to the words churning inside your head. Repeat them aloud or write them down, if that will help capture them.

2. *Isolate destructive words and phrases.* Fran's inner voice kept telling her she was "only a secretary." Mark's reminded him he was "just a salesman." With the word *only or just*, they were downgrading their jobs and, by extension, themselves.

诉我我被调离了，他说这是提升，可是如果我做得很好为什么要让我走呢？"

随后，苏又逐渐转移了话题，提及两年前她获得了 MBU 学位，还有一份相当高的薪水，这听起来可决不像个失败者。

第一次治疗结束时，苏的医生让她把自己的想法写出来，尤其是在晚上睡不着的时候。在第二次会诊时，苏的纸上写着，"我并不精明。""在我面前有一大堆倒霉事。""明天对我来说就是一个灾难。""我以前从未组织过一次会议。""老板今天早上看起来很生气，我该怎么办？"

她承认仅一天就能列出 26 条悲观想法，难怪总是觉得很累很沮丧。

当苏听到自己的担心和猜疑被大声念出来后，她突然意识到太多的精力被自己浪费在假想的灾难当中。如果你一直感到情绪低落，这可能是你自己给自己制造的麻烦。倾听那些缠绕在你脑海中的声音，大声地重复或写下来，也许这样会对你有所帮助。

2. 别让消极词乘虚而入。弗兰的心里一直有一个声音在不断提醒她："你仅仅是一个秘书。"马克总是想着自己不过是一个销售员。就是这些"不过"和"仅仅"就让他们看轻了自己的职业，更进一步看轻了自己。

❹ **squander**
/ˈskwɒndə/
v. 浪费

❺ **catastrophe**
/kəˈtæstrəfɪ/
n. 灾难

By isolating negative words and phrases, you can pinpoint the damage you're doing to yourself. For Fran and Mark, the culprits[6] were *only* and *just*. Once those words are eliminated, there's nothing destructive about saying "I am a salesman" or "I am a secretary." Both statements open doors to positive follow-ups, such as, "I'm on my way up the ladder."

3. *Stop the thought*. Short-circuit negative messages as soon as they start by using the one-word command stop!

   "What will I do if..." *stop*!

   In theory, stopping is a simple technique. In practice, it's not as easy as it sounds. To be effective at stopping, you have to be forceful and tenacious[7]. Raise your voice when you give the command. Picture yourself drowning out the inner voice of fear.

4. *Accentuate*[8] *the positive*. There's a story about a man who went to a psychiatrist, "What's the trouble?" asked the doctor.

   "Two months ago my grandfather died and left me $75,000. Last month, a cousin passed away and left me $100,000."

   "Then why are you depressed?"

   "This month, *nothing*!"

   When a person is in a depressed mood, everything can seem

隔绝这些消极语素你就能清楚地看到这些事情的危害性。对于弗兰和马克来说，这些"不过"和"仅仅"就是罪魁祸首。摆脱了它们，对自己说"我是一个秘书"，"我是一个销售员"，是不会构成任何伤害的。这样说带来的是积极向上的想法，诸如"我会更上一层楼"。

3.向悲观的想法喊"停"。阻断负面的信息，一旦他们开始影响你的时候，立即喊停。杜绝那些"要是……我怎么办？"的想法。

理论上，喊停是再简单不过的，可实际操作起来就不像听起来那么容易了。善于此道的人必须是坚韧而有力的。当你喊停的时候一定要提高音量，想像着把内心深处的恐惧驱逐出去。

4.更加乐观。有这样一个故事，一个人去看心理医生，医生问他："你怎么了？"

"两个月前，我的祖父去世了，留给我7万5千美元。上个月，我堂兄也去世了，留给我10万美元。"

"那你还有什么可抱怨的。"

"这个月，什么都没了。"

当一个人非常沮丧时，他看任何事情都会很悲观。所以当你赶走心中的消极思想时，就要用积极向上的思想来取代它。

❻ **culprit**
/ˈkʌlprɪt/
n. 引起不良后果的事物
❼ **tenacious**
/tɪˈneɪʃəs/
adj. 固执的，顽强
❽ **accentuate**
/ækˈsentjueɪt/
v. 着重强调

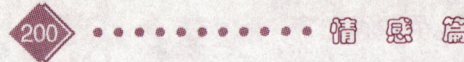

depressing. So once you've exorcised the demons by calling a stop, replace them with good thoughts.

5. *Reorient*[9] *yourself*. Have you ever been feeling down late in the day, when someone suddenly said, "Let's go out." Remember how your spirits picked up? You changed the direction of your thinking, and your mood brightened.

5. 重新定位你自己：在一天结束的时候，你是否会觉得情绪很低落，这时如果有人突然提出"我们出去吧"，还记得你是如何变得兴高采烈吗？把思维的方向转换一下，你就会振奋起来。

❾ **reorient**
/ˈriːˈɔːrɪent/
v. 再定方向

Learning to accept yourself
学会接受你自己

The world's heaviest burden is a great potential.

世界最大的负担就是潜在的担忧。

We are not born doubting ourselves. We learn to do it. In fact, we are usually taught to doubt ourselves. Often we are taught to do so by otherwise well-meaning people who are passing along their own doubts and uncertainties and who believe they are being protective and caring. What these people (usually parents and other significant adults) want are strong, capable and self-confident people, but they often inadvertently[1] teach us thought processes that lead to something else. That's the bad news. The good news is that we can understand some of these processes and learn new ways of coping that allow us to become more accepting of ourselves. Following are six behaviors you may have learned that can be unlearned and allow you to move toward greater self-acceptance.

Moralistic[2] Self-Judgment

One way to really dislike yourself is to always judge yourself in a very moralistic way. People often spend a lot of time and energy labeling their behavior with moral adjectives such as "bad," "hateful" and "mean." When you apply these kinds of words to yourself you make liking yourself much more difficult. There is a more productive way of looking at yourself that will allow you to begin to like yourself more. Instead of evaluating yourself in this moralistic way, begin to ask questions like: "Did I do what I really wanted to do in this situation?" "How can I correct the misunderstanding that occurred?" In other words, you can start to view what you've done as productive or non-productive rather than as good or bad. If something is non-productive, you can focus on what you have learned from it and try another approach that might

我们并不是天生就怀疑自己，而是学来的。实际上，我们被人教育去怀疑自己，这些人要么正在经历他自己的麻烦和不确定的事情，要么就是相信自己是出于保护和同情心的。他们（通常是父母和其他重要的长辈）本意是希望我们能成为强壮的、有能力的和自信的人，但是他们的教导方式不经意间常常会导致其他的结果。那是一个坏事情。但是可喜的是我们可以理解他们的用心并且通过学习新的方式让我们变得能接受自己。下面是六种你可能已经学会的但可以抛弃的行为，通过介绍可以让你更加接受你自己。

自责

现实中不喜欢自己的一种情况就是用教训的方式来判断自己。人们经常花大量的时间和精力用"差的"、"可恶的"、"低劣的"这些词来形容自己，但是当你这样做的时候，你就会变得很难喜欢自己。有一种看待自己的方式可以让你变得更喜欢自己。不是用那些教训的方式来评价自己，而是开始问自己一些问题，比如"在这种情况下，我做了自己真正想做的事情吗？""我怎样能消除误解？"换句话说，你开始用是否有成效来判断自己做的事情，而不是用好事或者坏事评价。如果有些事情的效果不好，你可以将

❶ **inadvertently**
/ˌɪnətˈvɜːtəntlɪ/
adv. 漫不经心地

❷ **moralistic**
/ˌmɒrəˈlɪstɪk/
adj. 说教的

be more productive.

Over-Generalizing

Another thing that might cause you not to accept yourself is over-generalizing about something you've done that you don't like. So, for example, if you fail a test you might generalize and say, "I'm really a stupid person." When you do this you are making a statement about all of you all of the time and not just about this one situation at this time. Instead, you might decide that your grade on this test in this subject at this time was indeed poor, and then go on to decide what you want to do about your poor grade, if anything. Getting stuck in over-generalizing discourages you from taking steps that might allow you to do better on the next exam and builds an expectation of future failure.

Impossibly High Standards

Having standards that are impossibly high is a third way you can not accept yourself. It may not come as a surprise to you that most of us are more demanding[3] of ourselves than we are of others. Somehow we can tolerate the fact that other people fail, that they aren't always kind, that they've done things they aren't proud of, but we have difficulty accepting those very human aspects of ourselves. The need to be perfect is another way to set yourself up for failure and enhance[4] the feeling that you are not acceptable. We all make mistakes. Accepting less than perfection simply means recognizing the limitations inherent[5] in being born a human being. Learn to value who you are rather than who you could become. To quote Linus, a sober and often worried charac-

重点放在研究它并寻求另外的更好的办法上。

以偏概全

另一种导致你不能接受自己的情况是你对一件你已经做了但是又不喜欢做的事情的概括。比如，假如你有一次考试不及格，你可能就会说："我真是一个愚蠢的人。"当你下这个结论的时候，不是针对这段时间的这次考试而是对你自己和全部时间而下的结论。这样你就不会将注意力放在你这个科目的这次考试中的分数上从而在这方面改进。总之，过分的概括将会打消你的积极性，使你在下一次的考试中不能考的更好和建立信心。

不现实的目标

第三种情况是对自己要求太高了。不可否认，我们大多数人都更看重自己，不知道为什么我们总是能够容忍别人的失败，但是当自己面对时却很难接受。人们追求完美的需求是另一种导致自己感到失败和不能接受自己的情况。每个人都会犯错误，我们应该认识到人与生俱来的局限性，学会用你是谁而不是你能变成谁来评价自己。引用莱纳斯，一部流行的戏剧中一个镇定并经常感到担忧的角色的话来说就是，"世界最大的负担就是潜在的担忧"。如果我们总是做我们想当然的

❸ **demanding**
/dɪˈmɑːdɪŋ/
adj. 要求严格的

❹ **enhance**
/ɪnˈhɑːns/
v. 提高，增加

❺ **inherent**
/ɪnˈhɪərənt/
adj. 生来俱有的，内在的

ter from a popular comic strip, "The world's heaviest burden is a great potential." Wouldn't it be overwhelming if we always had to do what we imagine we could do? Nobody has the time and energy to do all of that. We must make choices about what we will pursue and do them the best we can under the circumstances (which aren't always ideal, by the way).

Not accepting that there are Real Limits to Your Abilities

The idea that you should always be able to attain[6] your goals as long as you work hard enough is another factor interfering with self-acceptance. You will reach many of your goals and should give yourself credit for having done so. Some of us have trouble seeing our successes because we focus so much on our failures and many times the failures come after a lot of hard work and personal suffering. It seems that all that hard work should pay off in our having reaching the goal we set out to achieve. It is hard to accept that a given goal may be out of our reach and that may be because of many factors, including the fact that we may not have the talent or skill needed to reach the goal. Of course there may be other factors in operation that make the achieving of that goal at that time impossible — health concerns, financial problems, family difficulties, extraneous[7] stressors, or any number of other factors acting alone or together. The real trick to self-acceptance is to see that the goal is unattainable, at least for now, and shifting your focus to accomplishing what you can accomplish under the circumstances. That could include evaluating your original goal and deciding whether or not to continue with it. It also means giving yourself credit for what you have accomplished and what

事情，那结果将是不可想像的，没有人有时间和精力去做所有事情。我们必须要有所选择。选择那些我们必须要做的事，和完成他们最好的时机（顺便说一下，这些条件不一定是理想的）。

不能接受你能力有限的事实

那种认为只要工作足够努力就一定能达到目标的想法是妨碍自我接受的另一个因素。我们可以达到很多的目标，通过实现它们可以建立信心。有些人却看不到成功因为我们总是把注意力集中于我们的失败，尤其是当好多次在经历了大量的辛勤劳动和个人受了很多苦后得到的还是失败时。看起来我们所有的努力都白费了，我们很难接受这样的事实：我们未能达到目标可能是由许多因素造成的，包括我们没有那方面的天分和完成目标所需要的技术等。当然可能还有其他一些操作上的因素——健康、经济问题、家庭困难、外来的刺激，或者许多其他单个因素或多个因素综合作用的结果。真正自我接受的关键在于要意识到这个目标是不可实现的，至少现在是不可实现的。转移你的重点到一个在现有条件下能完成的目标上。这可能包括评估你原来的目标并决定是否继续将它做下去，也意味着你能从你所能完成

❻ attain
/əˈteɪn/
v. 达到，成为

❼ extraneous
/eksˈtreɪnjəs/
adj. 外来的，无关系的

you have learned from your experiences.

The Comparison Trap

Judging yourself by what others have accomplished is a sure way to lower your self-acceptance. Have you noticed that you never compare yourself to people who seem to aspire[8] to less than you do and that you always chose those people who are the top performers or the most popular as your yardstick[9] for success? Are you as good as your friends, you brother or sister, your parents or Joe Blow? And how about trying to be like "normal" people are? (And who or what determines what is "normal"?) Can you only be good if you're better than someone else? When we use other people as our yardstick, we aren't taking into consideration our own personal limitations or talents. For example, if someone seems to be more articulate[10] than you, you can respond in one of two ways: You can become upset and depressed by telling yourself that you should be as articulate as that person, or you can recognize and accept the fact that there are probably a lot of people out there who are more articulate than you at certain times and under certain circumstances and that is OK. It doesn't mean a thing about you. Playing the comparison game is a dead end street. By doing that you are probably missing some other qualities by which you can judge your own worth, like your honesty, friendliness, caring nature, dedication and so forth. And really, people don't value you for how much you are like someone else. They do value you for the ways you are being you.

的和你能从你的经验中学来的东西上建立信心。

攀比

根据别人所做的来判断你自己也是一个降低自我接受的因素。你是否注意到你从来不会拿自己和不如你的人来比较而总是和那些最优秀的或最流行的人来比呢？你和你的朋友、你的兄弟姐妹、你的父母或者其他人一样好吗？做一个普通人怎么样呢？（什么是"普通"呢？），比别人好就真的能称之为好吗？当我们把别人作为标准的时候，并没有考虑我们个人的缺陷或者天分。例如，某个人比你能说会道，你可能会有两种反应，要么你开始变得不安和沮丧，并告诉自己你要有那个人一样的好口才，或者你能够认识并接受这个事实，可能有许多人在特定的时间和场合比你的口才好，这没什么。玩这种比较游戏是死路一条。它可能会导致你忘记自己的其他一些品质，诸如诚实、友善、同情心等。实际上人们并不会评价你多么像另一个人。而是你怎么来实现自己的价值。

❽ **aspire**
/əsˈpaɪə/
v. 热望，立志

❾ **yardstick**
/ˈjɑːdstɪk/
n. 准绳

❿ **articulate**
/ɑːˈtɪkjʊlət/
adj. 善于表达的，口才好的

Passivity

Just passively letting your life happen may make it more difficult to accept yourself. Part of accepting yourself is engaging in activities that help you like yourself. Think back to those times when you weren't concerned about your acceptability[11]. What kinds of things were you doing? How were you spending your time? To accept and like yourself means that you approve of how you are living your life. If you aren't accepting yourself, you probably don't like the activities you're engaged in. You are feeling dissatisfied. A way to increase your self-acceptance is to become more actively engaged in your life. Look for those activities and relationships that give you the most enjoyment — not necessarily the most enjoyment you could possibly have, but the most you can get from your choices at the moment. Try new things, perhaps things you have always wanted to try but didn't because you felt you couldn't do them. Try them with the attitude that you want to know what it would actually be like to do them. You may find that they are enjoyable and that you want to continue them. You may find that they are OK, but not worth continuing. You may find that you don't like them at all and feel fine about crossing them off your list of things to do. Trying and getting real experience is a way of feeling better about yourself and gaining more confidence in your abilities.

被动

正是由于被动才让你的变得很难接受你自己。你所热中的事情能帮助你接受自己。回想一下你不能接受自己的那些时候，你正在做什么事情？你在怎样度过你的时间？接受并喜欢上自己就意味着赞成你现在的生活方式。如果你不接受自己，你就可能不喜欢你正在从事的事情，你感到不满意。增加你的自我接受度的一个办法就是使自己在生活中更积极一些。寻找那些最能令你感到高兴的事情或者关系。尝试新的事物，那些你曾想尝试但是因为你不自信而没有做的事，带着一种想知道它到底是怎么回事的态度去尝试。你可能就会发现他们是令人愉快的并且你想要继续下去；也可能发现它们很好，但是不值得继续下去；当然你也可能根本就不喜欢它们，并且放弃。尝试并实际操作是一个很好的办法，它可以让你对自己感觉更好并对自己的能力更加有信心。

⓫ acceptability
/əkˌseptəˈbɪlɪtɪ/
n. 可接受性

The doll and a white rose
布娃娃和一枝白玫瑰

I left there in tears; my life changed forever.

我流着眼泪离开了那儿,从此我对生活的看法改变了很多。

I hurried into the local department store to grab some last minute Christmas gifts, I looked at all the people and grumbled[1] to myself. I would be in here forever and I just had so much to do.

Christmas was beginning to become such a drag. I kind of wished that I could just sleep through Christmas. But I hurried the best I could through all the people to the toy department.

Once again I kind of mumbled[2] to myself at the prices of all these toys. And wondered if the grandkids would even play with them. I found myself in the doll aisle[3]. Out of the corner of my eye I saw a little boy about 5 holding a lovely doll. He kept touching her hair and he held her so gently. I wondered who the doll was for. I watched him turn to a woman and he called his aunt by name and said, "Are you sure I don't have enough money?" She replied a bit impatiently, "You know that you don't have enough money for it." The aunt told the lithe[4] boy not to go anywhere that she had to go get some other things and would be back in a few minutes. And then she left the aisle. The boy continued to hold the doll. After a bit I asked the boy who the doll was for. "It is the doll my sister wanted so badly for Christmas. She just knew that Santa would bring it." I told him that maybe Santa was going to bring it. "No, Santa can't go where my sister is ... I have to give the doll to my Mamma to take to her." I asked him where his sister was. He looked at me with the saddest eyes and said, "She was gone to be with Jesus. My Daddy says that Mamma is going to have to go to be with her."

布娃娃和一枝白玫瑰

最后一刻，我冲进商店去购买圣诞礼物，看看满屋的顾客，我开始埋怨自己。买东西可能要花费很长时间，而我有好多事情要做。

圣诞似乎正在成为一种累赘，我真希望圣诞期间可以大睡几天。但是我还是要去那拥挤不堪的玩具店。

我开始咕哝这些玩具的价格，而且怀疑孩子们到底喜不喜欢玩这类玩具，我来到了卖布娃娃的专区，我用眼一瞟，看到了一个大约五岁的小男孩正捧着一个非常可爱的布娃娃，他轻轻地抱着布娃娃，不断地摸着布娃娃的头发。我想知道那个布娃娃是给谁的。我看到他转向一个女士，并叫她姑姑的名字："你确定我们的钱不够？"她有一点儿不耐烦的说："你买不起那个布娃娃。"她还有别的东西要买，过一会儿才能回来，所以告诉他不要乱跑。之后，她离开了布娃娃专柜。小男孩仍旧抱着布娃娃，过了一会儿我前去问他，布娃娃想送给谁。"这是我小妹妹希望在圣诞节得到的礼物，她知道圣诞老人会把这个礼物送给她的。"我告诉他说不定圣诞老人会把这个布娃娃送给他的小妹妹。"永远不会了，圣诞老人去不了她住的地方……我只有把布娃娃送给妈妈，让她给妹妹捎去。"我问他的妹妹在哪儿，他无限悲伤的看着我说："她和上帝在一起，爸爸说妈妈也要去

❶ grumble
/ˈɡrʌmbl/
v. 抱怨

❷ mumble
/ˈmʌmbl/
v. 咕哝

❸ aisle
/aɪl/
n. 过道，通道

❹ lithe
/laɪð/
adj. 柔软的

My heart nearly stopped beating. Then the boy looked at me again and said, "I told my Daddy to tell Mamma not to go yet. I told him to tell her to wait till I got back from the store." Then he asked me if I wanted to see his picture. I told him I would love to. He pulled out some pictures he'd taken at the front of the store. "I want my Mamma to take this with her so she won't ever forget me. But daddy says she will need to be with my sister." I saw that the little boy had lowered his head. While he was not looking I reached into my purse and pulled out a handful of bills. I asked the little boy, "Shall we count that money one more time?" He grew excited and said, "Yes, I just know it has to be enough," So I slipped[5] my money in with his and we began to count it. Of course it was plenty for the doll. He softly said, "Thank you Jesus for giving me enough money. Then the boy said, "I just asked Jesus to give me enough money to buy this doll, so Mamma can take it with her to give to my sister. And he heard my prayers. I wanted to ask him for enough to buy my Mamma a white rose, but I didn't ask him, but he gave me enough to buy the doll and a rose for my Mamma. She loves white roses so very, very much."

In a few minutes the aunt came back and I wheeled my cart away. I could not keep from thinking about the little boy as I finished my shopping in a totally different spirit than when I had started. And I kept remembering a story I had seen in the newspaper several days earlier about a drunk driver hitting a car and killing a little girl and the Mother was in serious condition. The family was deciding on whether to remove[6] the life support. Now surely this little boy did not belong with that story.

上帝那儿去陪妹妹了。"

　　我的心猛然一沉,接着小男孩看看我又对我说:"我和爸爸说让妈妈不要走,我让爸爸告诉妈妈等我从商店买回布娃娃她再走。"他问我愿不愿意看他的照片,我说愿意,他拿出一些在商店门前拍的照片给我看。"我想让妈妈带着这些,这样她就不会忘记我,但是爸爸说妈妈得和妹妹在一起。"小男孩慢慢低下了头,他没有看到我从自己的钱包里抄出了一叠钞票。我问他:"我们再数一下钱,好吗?"他非常激动地说:"好的,我知道钱一定够,"我悄悄地把这叠钱放到他的钱里,然后我俩一起开始数钱。男孩继续说道:"我刚才还在祈祷上帝赐给我足够的钱买下那个布娃娃,因为我想让妈妈把它带给小妹妹,啊,他听到了我的祈祷,本来我还想祈祷他赐给我更多的钱恰好再买一支白玫瑰,可我没有说,但是上帝赐给我的钱正够买到布娃娃和玫瑰,知道吗,我妈妈非常喜欢白玫瑰。"

　　过了一会儿,他的姑姑回来了,我推着购物车走开了。买完东西后,我禁不住又想起了那个小男孩,此时我的心境与刚刚购物时大不一样。这时,我想起了前几天在报纸上读到的一则消息:一酗酒司机撞死一个小女孩,女孩妈妈撞成重伤被送往医院,家属

❺ **slip**
/slɪp/
v. 塞入

❻ **remove**
/rɪ'muːv/
v. 移开,去除

Two days later I read in the paper where the family had disconnected[7] the life support and the young woman had died. I could not forget the little boy and just kept wondering if the two were somehow connected. Later that day, I could not help myself and I went out and bought some white roses and took them to the funeral home where the young woman was. And there she was holding a lovely white rose, the beautiful doll, and the picture of the little boy in the store. I left there in tears; my life changed forever.

正在决定要不要继续靠药物维持她的生命。当然这个小男孩不会属于那个故事。

  两天后,我在报纸上读到一则关于这个妇女的消息:她的家属决定不再通过药物继续维持她的生命,她已经与世长辞了。我真的无法忘记那个小男孩,而且总想知道这两件事是否有某种联系,最后我还是忍不住买了一些白玫瑰去了墓地。在她的墓前我看到了一支可爱的白玫瑰,一个漂亮的布娃娃,以及那张小男孩在商店的照片。我流着眼泪离开了那儿,从此我对生活的看法改变了很多。

7 disconnect
/ˌdɪskəˈnekt/
v. 拆开,分离

Best friends

最好的朋友

Never underestimate the power of your actions. With one small gesture you can change a person's life. For better or for worse.

不要低估你的行为。一个小小的举动,不论是好是坏,都可以改变一个人的一生。

One day, when I was a freshman in high school, I saw a kid from my class who was walking home from school. His name was Kyle. It looked like he was carrying all of his books. I thought to myself, "Why would anyone bring home all his books on a Friday? He must really be a nerd[1]."

I had quite a weekend planned (parties and a football game with my friends tomorrow afternoon), so I shrugged my shoulders and went on. As I was walking, I saw a bunch of kids running toward him. They ran at him, knocking all his books out of his arms and tripping[2] him so he landed in the dirt. His glasses went flying, and I saw them land in the grass about ten feet from him. He looked up and I saw this terrible sadness in his eyes. So, I jogged over to him and as he crawled[3] around looking for his glasses, and I saw a tear in his eye. As I handed him his glasses, I said, "Those guys are jerks[4]. They really should not get lives." He looked at me and said, "Hey thanks!" There was a big smile on his face. It was one of those smiles that showed real gratitude.

I helped him pick up his books, and asked him where he lived. As it turned out, he lived near me, so I asked him why I had never seen him before. He said he had gone to a private school before now. We talked all the way home, and I carried his books. He turned out to be a pretty cool kid. I asked him if he wanted to play football on Saturday with my friends and me. He said yes. The more I got to know Kyle, the more I liked him. And my friends thought the same of him.

最好的朋友

那年我还是高中新生。一天，看见我们班的同学凯尔，正搬着他所有的书回家，我暗自想道，"为什么在星期五搬这么多书啊？他一定是个书虫。"

我的周末计划得很好（聚会，明天下午和朋友去足球比赛），因此，我不屑地继续往前走。这时一群孩子向凯尔跑过来，他们把他撞倒了，书从他的手臂上掉了下来，他被绊倒在地。他的眼镜飞到了离他10英尺远的草地上，他抬起了头，我看到了他眼中那无限的悲哀。我小跑过去，当他在地上慢慢挪动着身体去找他的眼镜时，我看到了他眼里的泪水。我把眼镜捡回来，递给他说："这些蠢人，他们不得好死。"他看着我，脸上绽放出笑容，那是一种充满感激之情的微笑，然后对我说："谢谢。"

我帮他把书捡好，问他家住哪儿。原来，我们住的是那么近，问他为什么之前从没见过他，他回答说他一直上的是私立学校。我帮他拿着书，就这样我们聊了一路。其实，他是一个很酷的孩子。我问他愿不愿意在星期六和我还有我的朋友们一起去踢足球，他说愿意。我发现，越了解凯尔，就会越喜欢他，我的朋友们也有这种感觉。

星期一的早上，我又看到凯尔搬了一大

❶ **nerd**
/nɜːd/
n. 书虫

❷ **trip**
/trɪp/
v. 绊倒

❸ **crawl**
/krɔːl/
v. 爬行

❹ **jerk**
/dʒɜːk/
n. 蠢人

Monday morning came, and there was Kyle with the huge stack of books again. I stopped him and said, "Damn boy, you are gonna[5] really build some serious muscles with this pile of books everyday!" He just laughed and handed me half the books. Over the next four years, Kyle and I became best friends.

When we were seniors, we began to think about college. Kyle decided on Georgetown, and I was going to Duke. I knew that we would always be friends, that the miles would never be a problem.

Kyle was valedictorian[6] of our class. I teased him all the time about being a nerd. He had to prepare a speech for graduation. I was so glad it wasn't me having to get up there and speak. Graduation day, I saw Kyle. He looked great. He filled out and actually looked good in glasses. He had more dates than me and all the girls loved him!

Boy, sometimes I was jealous. Today was one of those days. I could see that he was nervous about his speech. So, I smacked him on the back and said, "Hey, big guy, you'll be great!" He looked at me with one of those looks (the really grateful one) and smiled. "Thanks," he said. As he started his speech, he cleared his throat, and began.

"Graduation is a time to thank those who helped you make it through those tough years. Your parents, your teachers, your siblings, maybe a coach...but mostly your friends. I am here to tell

摞书。我截住他，说道，"嗨，你每天都搬这么一大摞书，锻炼肌肉呀！"他只是笑笑，然后把一半书给了我。四年里，我和凯尔成了最要好的朋友。

四年级的时候，我们开始考虑考大学了。凯尔决定去 Georgetown 大学，而我决定去 Duke 大学，但我知道，距离不是问题，我们将是永远的朋友。

凯尔是我们班致告别辞的代表。我经常讥笑他是个书虫，他必须准备他的毕业讲话稿了。我很庆幸不是我站在那儿致毕业词。毕业那天，我看到了凯尔，他戴上眼镜显得那么英俊。他比我的约会多，所有的女孩子都喜欢他。

唉，有时，我还真的嫉妒他，今天也是。我可以看出他有点儿紧张，所以我拍了拍他的后背，说道："嗨，伙计，你一定能成的！"他还是以那种表情看着我（充满感激之情的表情），笑道："谢谢。"他清了清喉咙开始了他的演讲。

"毕业的时刻，要感谢那些所有帮助过你度过困境的人，包括你的父母、老师、兄弟、姐妹、教练……但是，最重要的要感谢你的朋友。这里我想说，友情是你可以给别人的最好礼物。接下来，我要给你们讲一个故

⑤ gonna
（口语）=going to

⑥ valedictorian
/ˌvælɪdɪkˈtɔːriən/
n. 致告别辞的毕业生代表

all of you that being a friend to someone is the best gift you can give him or her. I am going to tell you a story." I just looked at my friend with disbelief as he told the story of the first day we met. He had planned to kill himself over the weekend. He talked of how he had cleaned out his locker[7] so his mom wouldn't have to do it later and was carrying his stuff home. He looked hard at me and gave me a little smile. "Thankfully, I was saved. My friend saved me from doing the unspeakable."

I heard the gasp[8] go through the crowd as this handsome, popular boy told us all about his weakest moment. I saw his mom and dad looking at me and smiling that same grateful smile. Not until that moment did I realize it's depth.

Never underestimate[9] the power of your actions. With one small gesture you can change a person's life. For better or for worse.

事。"我简直不敢相信,他讲起了我们初次相遇的那一天。他讲道,那天,他计划好在周末自杀,他把他的橱柜彻底的清理干净,这样他妈妈就不用替他再清理了,那天他正在把所有东西往家运。他专注地看着我,露出了浅浅的微笑。"幸运的是,我被解救了,我的朋友把我从那难以启齿的罪恶中救出来了。"

人群中发出惊诧的喘息声,大家听着眼前这个英俊的,那么受欢迎的男生讲述着他生命中最脆弱的那一刻。我看到他的父母微笑地看着我,那一模一样的充满感激的微笑,直到那时我才明白那微笑的含义和深度。

不要低估你的行为。一个小小的举动,不论是好是坏,都可以改变一个人的一生。

7 locker
/ˈlɒkə/
n. 橱柜

8 gasp
/ɡɑːsp/
v. 喘息

9 underestimate
/ˌʌndəˈestɪmeɪt/
v. 低估

Love is memory
爱是记忆

Just as the sunset, their love was so strong and beautiful for one time but only destined to be a memory forever.

就像西沉的落日一样,他们一度如此强烈而美丽的爱注定只会成为永远的记忆。

情感篇

This is the first time for Erica and Bryan to have a date in another city, though it is only one hour away. Erica just felt a kind of release[1] for they don't have to take the pressure to meet someone knows them. For some reason, they have to keep it secrete.

It was really a nice day in late spring, warm and sunny. At first, Erica was not sure if everything would be working well or if they would have a good time. After all the business have been done, they found themselves were very hungry.

"What do you want to eat?" Erica asked.
"Anywhere you like, it is your birthday, and everything is your choice." Bryan smiled. It was not her birthday, but he always does this to tease[2] her.

Love in the Sunset.

They walked along the street and found a western restaurant.
"Let's eat here." Erica became a western food fan after she met Bryan.

That was a nice and clean restaurant, romantic to some extend. "Cheers!" Bryan raised his glass.

Erica found everything was perfect there, right for the mood she had at that time. They were eating, talking and laughing, just like a couple of happy lovers. Bryan picked up some of his food and put into Erica's mouth. Erica looked into his smiling eyes and felt that

爱是记忆

  这是埃里卡和布赖恩第一次在另一个城市约会，尽管只是一个小时的路程。埃里卡感到松了一口气，因为他们不用担心有人认识他们。因为某种原因，他们必须保守这个秘密。

  晚春的天气很好，温暖而晴朗。开始埃里卡还担心事情会不会进展顺利，或者他们是否会玩得开心。该做的事情做完以后，他们觉得饿了。

  "你想吃什么？"埃里卡问道。

  布赖恩笑着说："随便你，今天是你的生日，由你来决定。"今天并不是她的生日，但他总是这样说来逗她。

  夕阳之下，爱意浓浓。

  他们顺着街道走，找到一家西餐厅。

  "我们就在这吃吧。"埃里卡遇到布赖恩后就成了西餐迷。

  这家餐厅很干净，在某种程度上也很浪漫。"干杯！"布赖恩举起玻璃杯说。

  埃里卡发现那里的一切都很完美，正符合她当时的心情。他们边吃边聊、有说有笑，就像一对幸福的情侣。布赖恩夹了一些食物喂到埃里卡的嘴里。埃里卡看着他笑眯眯的眼睛，感觉自己完全沉浸在幸福中，像

❶ **release**
/rɪˈliːs/
n. 放松，释放

❷ **tease**
/tiːz/
v. 逗弄，取笑

she was totally overwhelmed[3]. Just like a dream! Later Erica ordered some ice cream, it was extremely sweet, deep into her heart.

"You are going to be a good father."

"Yes! But I may not be a good husband, because it is hard for me to be loyal."

Erica knew this is Bryan, his love is so unstable and that was definitely not only for one girl. Erica never asked what was role she played in his life, because she was afraid of the answer.

"What do you think? Are you going to be a good mother and a good wife?"

"I don't know!" Erica answered quickly.

Yes, everything changed since she fell in love with Bryan. Before that, Erica only believed in the love that is self-fish and mutual. She cannot bear share love with others. However, now, when she fell in love with Bryan she began to accept a kind of dangerous love, which may be hurt but really strong, she and her ex-boyfriend[4] broke up[5] and she decided to love Bryan all heart and soul.

"I am also not loyal, because I fell in love with you when I still with my ex-boyfriend. But my love is loyal, because I can only love one person at one time, even in only a short period." This is the first time Erica talked about her love.

"You are already my girlfriend! ..."

梦一样。后来埃里卡要了一些冰激凌，真甜，甜到心里。

"你会成为一个好父亲。"

"是的，但是我可能成不了好丈夫，因为对我来说专一很难。"

埃里卡知道这就是布赖恩，他的爱不专一，绝对不会只对一个女孩。埃里卡从来没问她在他生活中扮演什么角色，因为她害怕听到答案。

"你呢？你会成为一个好母亲，好妻子吗？"

"我不知道。"埃里卡回答得很快。

是的，自从爱上布赖恩后，一切都变了。在这以前埃里卡只相信爱情是自私的、相互的，她不能和别人分享爱情。然而现在，爱上布赖恩后她开始接受一种危险的爱。这种爱伤人但的确很强烈。和前任男友分开后，她决定全身心地爱布赖恩。

"我也不忠诚，因为我和你恋爱的同时，也和前任男友约会，但是我的爱是专一的，因为我一段时间只能爱一个人，即使时间很短。"这是埃里卡第一次谈爱。

"你已经是我的女友了！……"

❸ overwhelm
/ˌəʊvəˈwelm/
v. 沉浸

❹ ex-boyfriend
/ˈeksˈbɔɪfrend/
n. 前任男友

❺ break up
分开，分手

Bryan said a lot, but Erica only got this sentence. This meant a lot to her, she was expecting this for quite a long time. No matter it was true or not, she was deeply moved.

After they finished the dinner, they decided to go to the park. Beautiful spring and romantic place! Erica has been to the park for many times, but only this time, she found everything was different. All the flowers seemed smiled at her and the petal[6] was dancing with the wind, together with the fragrant air. The park was right a fairyland[7] to Erica.

It was almost the dusk. So there were not too many visitors. Erica and Bryan chose to walk though the small alleys[8] with few people. They chasing and laughing, Erica found that this was the most romantic date ever.

"Oh, let's choose a viewpoint to watch the sunset." Bryan suggested.

They finally sat on the beach of the lake, and right in front of them the sun was setting behind the mountain. The final sunlight sprinkled[9] on the lake, which was exactly like a golden mirror. They sat there without a word. Suddenly, Erica's phone began to ring. She checked the number and it was her ex-boyfriend. It seems that every time when she enjoyed the special moments with Bryan, her ex-boyfriend would ruin it, though it is always just the coincidence in time.

布赖恩说了很多，埃里卡只记住了这一句。这对她来说意味着很多，她盼这句话盼了很长时间了。不管是真是假，她都深深地被感动了。

他们吃完晚饭后，决定去公园。美丽的春天，浪漫的地方。埃里卡来这个公园很多次了，但是这一次，她发现一切都不同了。所有的花都朝她笑，花瓣也随风起舞，散发着香味。对埃里卡来说，这个公园就是仙境。

接近黄昏了，游客不多，埃里卡和布赖恩沿着没什么人的小夹道继续走着。他们互相追赶、欢笑。埃里卡觉得这是最浪漫的一天。

"我们找个地方欣赏落日吧。"布赖恩建议说。

最后他们坐在湖边，正对着太阳落山的地方。落日的余辉洒在湖面上，就像一面金色的镜子。他们坐着没说一句话，突然埃里卡的手机响了，她看了看号码，是她前任男友打来的。似乎每一次她和布赖恩享受美妙时刻时，她的前任男友都要捣乱，尽管这只是偶然。

布赖恩也听到铃声，突然他紧紧地握住埃里卡的手。埃里卡很吃惊，因为布赖恩从

❻ **petal**
/ˈpetl/
n. 花瓣

❼ **fairyland**
/ˈfeərɪlænd/
n. 仙境

❽ **alley**
/ˈælɪ/
n. 小巷，胡同

❾ **sprinkle**
/ˈsprɪŋkl/
v. 洒

Bryan also heard the ring, suddenly, he put his hand on Erica's hand holding tightly. Erica was shocked for that Bryan never held her hand or even never touched her in public. Erica was trembling and looked at Bryan in his eyes, which was saying something. Bryan has really charming and passionate eyes, as blue and deep as the sea. She always avoided his sight because she would totally lost in his eyes. But this time, Erica would rather lose. She shut off the phone.

Then Bryan just hugged her on the waist, without a word, Erica felt she was drunk for everything around her. She did wish that time would just be froze at that moment. The sun was still sinking, and finally disappeared behind the mountain.

"It's gone!" Bryan said with smile.
"Will it be back again." Erica uttered the stupid question.
"Of course! Tomorrow morning, if god permits." Bryan answered.

"Everything has a beginning and has an end." Erica repeated this sentence in her brain again and again. She clearly knew that, this would be the perfect description of their love. Bryan will leave in a few months and they may not see each other again after that. Just as the sunset, their love was so strong and beautiful for one time but only destined[10] to be a memory forever.

来没握过她的手,也从来没在公共场合碰过她。埃里卡颤动着,看着布赖恩会说话的眼睛。布赖恩的眼睛真的很迷人,充满激情,像海一样蓝、一样深。她总是避开他的眼睛,因为她会完全迷失在他的眼睛里。但是这次,埃里卡宁愿迷失,她挂断了电话。布赖恩只是搂着她的腰,什么话也没说。埃里卡陶醉于周围的一切,她真希望时间在那个时候凝住。太阳还在下沉,最后消失在山后。

"太阳不见了。"布赖恩笑着说。

"它还会升起来吗?"埃里卡问了这么傻的一个问题。

布赖恩答道:"当然,如果上帝允许,明早会升起来的。"

"一切都有始有终。"埃里卡一遍又一遍地在脑中重复这句话。她清楚地知道这是对他们的爱的最好描述。布赖恩几个月后要离开,那以后他们再也不会相见了。就像西沉的落日一样,他们一度如此强烈而美丽的爱注定只会成为永远的记忆。

❿ **destine**
/ˈdestɪn/
v. 注定

Salty coffee
咸咖啡

A man who can admit that he's homesick must love his home and care about his family. He must be responsible.

一个想家的男人一定很爱家,很在乎家,他一定很有责任感。

情感篇

He met her at a party. She was outstanding; many guys were after her, but nobody paid any attention to him. After the party, he invited her for coffee. She was surprised. So as not to appear rude, she went along.

As they sat in a nice coffee shop, he was too nervous[1] to say anything and she felt uncomfortable. Suddenly, he asked the waiter, "Could you please give me some salt? I'd like to put it in my coffee."

They stared[2] at him. He turned red, but when the salt came, he put it in his coffee and drank. Curious, she asked, "Why salt with coffee?" He explained[3], "When I was a little boy, I lived near the sea. I liked playing in the sea ... I could feel its taste salty, like salty coffee. Now every time I drink it, I think of my childhood and my hometown. I miss it and my parents, who are still there."

She was deeply touched[4]. A man who can admit that he's homesick[5] must love his home and care about his family. He must be responsible.

She talked too, about her faraway hometown, her childhood, her family. That was the start to their love story.

They continued to date. She found that he met all her requirements. He was tolerant[6], kind, warm and careful. And to think she would have missed the catch if not for the salty coffee!

咸咖啡

他在晚会上遇见了她，她很出众，有很多男孩追求，但没有人注意到他。晚会结束后，他邀请她去喝咖啡，她很吃惊。但为了不至于不礼貌，她去了。

他们坐在一家精致的咖啡店，他很紧张，一句话也说不出来，她感到很不舒服。突然他叫来服务生说："请给我一些盐，我想放在咖啡里。"

他们盯着他，他脸红了。盐端上来了，他放了一些在咖啡里，开始喝。她很好奇地问："为什么加盐？"他解释说："我儿时住在海边，我喜欢在海里玩，我能尝到它的咸味，就像咸咖啡。现在每当我喝咖啡时我就想起我的童年和故乡。我想念它，想念现在还住在那儿的爸爸妈妈。"

她被深深地感动了。一个想家的男人一定很爱家，很在乎家，他一定很有责任感。

她也谈到了她遥远的家乡、她的童年和家庭。就这样他们开始恋爱了。

他们继续约会，她发现他能达到她所有的标准和要求，他很宽容、友好、真诚、细心。她甚至想如果不是一杯咸咖啡，她可能不会理他。

❶ **nervous**
/ˈnɜːvəs/
adj. 紧张的
❷ **stare**
/ˈsteər/
v. 盯着看
❸ **explain**
/ɪksˈpleɪn/
v. 解释
❹ **touched**
/tʌtʃt/
adj. 感动的
❺ **homesick**
/ˈhəʊmsɪk/
adj. 想家的
❻ **tolerant**
/ˈtɒlərənt/
adj. 容忍的

So they married and lived happily together. And every time she made coffee for him, she put in some salt, the way he liked it.

After 40 years, he passed away and left her a letter which said:

My dearest, please forgive my life-long lie. Remember the first time we dated? I was so nervous I asked for salt instead of[7] sugar[8].

It was hard for me to ask for a change, so I just went ahead. I never thought that we would hit it off. Many times, I tried to tell you the truth, but I was afraid that it would ruin everything.

Sweetheart, I don't exactly like salty coffee. But as it mattered so much to you, I've learnt to enjoy it. Having you with me was my greatest happiness. If I could live a second time, I hope we can be together again, even if it means that I have to drink salty coffee for the rest of my life.

咸咖啡

他们结婚了，生活得很幸福。每一次她给他煮咖啡都要放些盐，因为他喜欢。

40年后，他去世了，给她留了一封信：

亲爱的，请原谅我瞒了你一生的谎言。还记得我们第一次约会吗？我很紧张，本来我想要糖的，我却要了盐。

再改对我来说太难了，于是我将错就错。我从来没想我们要喝咸咖啡，很多次我想告诉你真相，但我担心说出来后一切都会被破坏。

亲爱的，我其实并不喜欢咸咖啡，但是既然那对你来说那么重要，我已经学会了享受它。和你在一起是我最大的幸福。如果我能再活一次，我希望我们还能在一起，即使那意味着我的余生都必须喝咸咖啡。

❼ **instead of**
代替
❽ **sugar**
/ˈʃʊgə/
n. 糖

Test of true love
真爱的考验

Dear, I have my answer. I will never pick the flower for you if it meant certain death.

亲爱的，我有答案了。如果必死无疑的话，我是不会去采那朵花的。

My husband is an engineer. Since the day we met, he has always been the rock in my life. I knew he had his feet firmly planted on the ground, and it seemed that no matter what else went crazy, he would be the one constant.

Three years of romance and two years of marriage later, I tired of him. He is the most unromantic man I know. He never bought me flowers, he never surprised me, and nothing had changed in our marriage.

After some time, I finally found the courage to tell him that I wanted out. He just sat there, speechless. My heart froze: what kind of man was I married to who didn't even know what to say to make me stay? After a while, he spoke. "What can I do to change your mind?"

"I will stay if you can give me a good answer to this question," I replied coldly. "If I asked for a flower that grew on a cliff[1], and you knew that getting it for me meant certain death, would you still get it for me?"

His face grew troubled[2]. "Can I give you the answer tomorrow morning?" With that, my heart sank. I knew that I could never be happy with a man who couldn't even give me an answer straight away.

The next morning, when I woke up, he was missing. In the living room, under a warm glass of milk, was a note. My eyes

真爱的考验

我丈夫是个工程师。自从我们相遇，他一直是我生命中可依赖的靠山。我知道他很务实，好像不管其他人变得多么疯狂，他都能一如既往地做自己的事。

三年的恋爱，两年的婚姻生活之后，我渐渐厌倦了他。他是我知道的最不浪漫的人，他从不买花给我，也不给我惊喜。我们的婚姻生活从来没有什么变化。

一段时间过后，我终于鼓起勇气告诉他我想离开。他只是坐在那里不说话。我的心凉了：跟我结婚的人怎么是这样的啊，他甚至不知道说些让我留下的话。过了一会他说："我能做些什么让你改变主意呢？"

"如果你能对这个问题给我一个满意的答案，我就留下。"我冷冷地说："如果我要一朵生长在峭壁上的鲜花，你也知道上那儿采花意味着死亡，你愿意为我采吗？"

他一脸苦相地说："我能明早给你答案吗？"听到这话，我的心往下沉了。我明白和这样一个都不能直接给我答案的人一起生活不会让我幸福。

第二天早上，我醒来的时候没看见他。客厅里，一杯热牛奶的底下放了一张纸条。我读着读着眼睛模糊了。

❶ cliff
/klɪf/
n. 峭壁

❷ troubled
/ˈtrʌbld/
adj. 苦恼的

grew misty as I read it.

"Dear, I have my answer. I will never pick the flower for you if it meant certain death.

But before you leave, I hope you will give me a chance to give you my reasons.

You always sit in front of the computer and type the whole day. But you always end up in tears because your format[3] goes <u>all over the place</u>[4]. I need my fingers to do the formatting for you, so that your tears will become smiles.

You like to travel but always get lost. I need my eyes to take you to the nicest places on earth. Every time you leave the house, you forget your keys. I need my legs to run home and open the door for you.

You never know how to take care of yourself. I need my hands to help you get rid of the pesky[5] white hair you hate so much when you grow old, to trim[6] your nails and to feed you.

So you see, that's why I cannot pick the flower for you. Until I find someone who loves you more than I do, I will need my body to take care of you.

"亲爱的,我有答案了。如果必死无疑的话,我是不会去采那朵花的。

但在你离开之前,我希望你能给我一个机会让我告诉你理由。

你经常坐在电脑前整天打字,但是最后你总是被气哭了,因为你的格式弄得乱七八糟。我需要用我的手指为你调整格式,把你的眼泪变成笑容。

你喜欢旅游,但经常迷路。我需要用我的眼睛带你到世界上最漂亮的地方去。每一次你离开家总是忘记带钥匙,我需要用我的腿跑回来为你开门。

你从不知道照顾自己。当你老了的时候,我需要用我的手帮你拔掉你那么憎恨的烦人的白头发,帮你修剪指甲,喂饭给你吃。

所以你看,这就是我不能为你采花的原因。在我找到一个比我更爱你的人之前,我需要用我的身体照顾你。

如果你接受了我的理由,请开门吧。我买了你最爱吃的松饼在等你。"

❸ **format**
/ˈfɔːmæt/
n. 格式

❹ **all over the place**
杂乱,紊乱

❺ **pesky**
/ˈpeskɪ/
adj. 烦人的

❻ **trim**
/trɪm/
v. 修剪

If you accept my reasons, then open the door and I will be waiting with your favorite[7] muffin[8]."

With tears streaming from my eyes, I opened the door. And there he was, with an extremely worried look on his face. He still had nothing to say; he just stood there, waving the packet he had in his hand in front of me.

I knew then that I would never find another man who will love me as much as my husband does.

Just because someone does not love you the way you want him to, it doesn't mean that he does not love you with all he has.

真爱的考验

我满脸泪水打开了门。他站在那儿，脸上显得很焦急。他还是没说什么，只是站在那，在我眼前晃了晃他手上的一包松饼。

那时我知道我再也找不到比我丈夫更爱我的人了。

仅仅是因为那个人不是以你想要的方式爱你，那并不意味着他不是全身心地爱你。

❼ **favorite**
/ˈfeɪvərɪt/
adj. 非常喜爱的

❽ **muffin**
/ˈmʌfɪn/
n. 松饼

For the love of mother
献给母爱

My mother was stone deaf and she could never hear me play during her life time.

我妈妈什么都听不见,她一辈子也不可能听到我的演奏。

When William, a 10-year old boy and somewhat scruffy[1] looking enrolled[2] himself to learn the piano, the music teacher was reluctant to accept him. She preferred her students to start their music lessons at a younger age when their fingers are nimble[3].

"William, why do you want to learn the piano?" the teacher asked. "I want to play for my mother." She noticed the tears in his eyes as he answered her. She had no heart to turn him down and accepted William as her student. But at each music lesson, William appeared to be in a hurry and played badly. "My mother is waiting outside for me," he would tell the teacher. She was tempted to advise William not to waste his time as he never hit the right note. But there was something about William, which she was fascinated with — the tender look of his eyes each time he mentioned "mother."

Suddenly, William stopped coming for his lessons. At the end of the semester year, the music teacher decided to organize a piano recital for her students and she sent flyers to them to participate. She was surprised to find William's application that he would like to contribute a musical piece. The music teacher was taken aback. She again had no heart to turn him down. She would put him as the last player in case he stumbled with his notes, she would come forward to remedy the situation.

The day came and William appeared with his hair uncombed and his shirt creased. He sat quietly with his eyes closed. When it was his turn to play, William bowed before the audience and said he

献给母爱

有点儿邋遢的10岁男孩威廉报名学钢琴时，音乐老师不愿意接收他。她想要年龄更小的学生，因为小孩子的手指更灵活。

"威廉，你为什么想学钢琴呢？"老师问。"我想弹给妈妈听。"她留意到他回答问题时眼里含着泪水。她不忍心打消他的积极性，所以，就把他收下了。但是，每次上音乐课时，威廉都显得很匆忙，弹得也很糟糕。他会告诉老师说："妈妈在外面等我。"她很想告诫威廉他是在浪费时间，因为他连一个音符都没有弹对过。但是，威廉身上有一种东西令她非常着迷——每次提到"妈妈"时他眼里那温柔的神情。

威廉突然不来上课了。老师决定在学年末组织一次学生钢琴独奏会，并发给他们一些练习曲目。当她发现威廉也要在独奏会上演奏一首曲子时，她很惊讶。音乐老师有点儿为难，但她又一次感到不忍心打消他的积极性。她会把他安排在最后演奏，万一他弹错了，她会上台补救。

到了演奏那一天，威廉来了，头发没有梳理，衬衫上也全是褶。他闭着眼睛静静地坐着。轮到他演奏时，他向观众鞠了一躬，并感谢音乐老师对他的耐心，因为他可能并不是她最出色的学生。

❶ scruffy
/ˈskrʌfɪ/
adj. 邋遢的

❷ enroll
/ɪnˈrəʊl/
v. 报名参加

❸ nimble
/ˈnɪmbl/
adj. 灵活的

was thankful for the music teacher's patience with him as he may not have been the best of her pupils.

"Tonight I am dedicating my music to my mother," he said. As he sat down and put his fingers on the keyboard, the most beautiful sound of music was heard. Everyone later asked why William did not bring his mother as she would surely be proud to hear him play.

William replied, "My mother was stone deaf and she could never hear me play during her life time. Yet she sacrificed[4] her time and money to let me learn the piano. This morning mother passed away. I am sure she is now happy as she can hear my piano recital. I chose a piece from Beethoven's concerto. As you all know, Beethoven was submerged with deafness at the triumph of his career. The piece symbolized his struggle for freedom from tyranny and released him from darkness and so was mother." Everyone was electrified[5] to hear what William said and tears welled over their eyes.

The music teacher proudly exclaimed, "William, not only your mother but we all are proud of you. We are deeply touched by your devotion and your love for mother," as she embraced him.

"今晚,我把我的音乐献给我的妈妈。"他说。他坐下来,手指触到键盘时,传出了最悠扬的音乐。后来,每个人都问威廉为什么没有带妈妈来。听到他的演奏,她一定会很自豪的。

威廉回答:"我妈妈什么都听不见,她一辈子也不可能听到我的演奏。但是,她却牺牲了自己的时间和金钱来让我学习弹钢琴。今天早上,妈妈走了。我相信她一定很高兴,因为她能够听到我的钢琴独奏了。我从贝多芬的协奏曲中选了一首曲子。你们都知道,贝多芬在他的事业的顶峰时期失聪了。这首曲子象征着他反对专制、争取自由的斗争,并将他从黑暗中解放了出来,对妈妈来说也是这样。"大家都被威廉的话和他如泉涌般的泪水所震动了。

音乐老师骄傲地说:"威廉,不仅你妈妈,还有我们大家也都以你为骄傲。你的孝心和对妈妈的爱深深地打动了我们。"说着,她拥抱了他。

❹ sacrifice
/ˈsækrɪfaɪs/
v. 牺牲

❺ electrify
/ɪˈlektrɪfaɪ/
v. 使震惊

图书在版编目（CIP）数据

英汉对照·心灵阅读. 3，情感篇/董新颖编译. —北京：外文出版社，2004
ISBN 7 – 119 – 03728 – 5

Ⅰ. 英… Ⅱ. 董… Ⅲ. 英语 – 对照读物 – 英、汉 Ⅳ. H319.4

中国版本图书馆 CIP 数据核字（2004）第 057581 号

外文出版社网址：
　http://www.flp.com.cn
外文出版社电子信箱：
　info@flp.com.cn
　sales@flp.com.cn

英汉对照·心灵阅读（三）

情　感　篇

编　译　董新颖
审　校　林立

责任编辑　王　蕊　李　溪
封面设计　时振晓
印刷监制　张国祥
出版发行　外文出版社
社　　址　北京市百万庄大街24号　邮政编码　100037
电　　话　(010) 68995963/5883（编辑部）
　　　　　(010) 68329514/68327211（推广发行部）
印　　刷　北京中印联印务有限公司
经　　销　新华书店/外文书店
开　　本　大32开　　　　　　　　字　数　150千字
印　　数　10001–15000册　　　　印　张　8.375
版　　次　2005年6月第1版第2次印刷
装　　别　平
书　　号　ISBN 7 – 119 – 03728 – 5/H · 1615（外）
定　　价　15.80元

版权所有　侵权必究